C000051690

SWEDISH
VOCABULARY

ENGLISH-
SWEDISH

The most useful words
To expand your lexicon and sharpen
your language skills

3000 words

Swedish vocabulary for English speakers - 3000 words

By Andrey Taranov

T&P Books vocabularies are intended for helping you learn, memorize and review foreign words. The dictionary is divided into themes, covering all major spheres of everyday activities, business, science, culture, etc.

The process of learning words using T&P Books' theme-based dictionaries gives you the following advantages:

- Correctly grouped source information predetermines success at subsequent stages of word memorization
- Availability of words derived from the same root allowing memorization of word units (rather than separate words)
- Small units of words facilitate the process of establishing associative links needed for consolidation of vocabulary
- Level of language knowledge can be estimated by the number of learned words

T&P Books Publishing
www.tpbooks.com

ISBN: 978-1-78071-311-3

This book is also available in E-book formats.
Please visit www.tpbooks.com or the major online bookstores.

SWEDISH VOCABULARY
for English speakers

T&P Books vocabularies are intended to help you learn, memorize, and review foreign words. The vocabulary contains over 3000 commonly used words arranged thematically.

- Vocabulary contains the most commonly used words
- Recommended as an addition to any language course
- Meets the needs of beginners and advanced learners of foreign languages
- Convenient for daily use, revision sessions, and self-testing activities
- Allows you to assess your vocabulary

Special features of the vocabulary

- Words are organized according to their meaning, not alphabetically
- Words are presented in three columns to facilitate the reviewing and self-testing processes
- Words in groups are divided into small blocks to facilitate the learning process
- The vocabulary offers a convenient and simple transcription of each foreign word

The vocabulary has 101 topics including:

Basic Concepts, Numbers, Colors, Months, Seasons, Units of Measurement, Clothing & Accessories, Food & Nutrition, Restaurant, Family Members, Relatives, Character, Feelings, Emotions, Diseases, City, Town, Sightseeing, Shopping, Money, House, Home, Office, Working in the Office, Import & Export, Marketing, Job Search, Sports, Education, Computer, Internet, Tools, Nature, Countries, Nationalities and more ...

T&P BOOKS' THEME-BASED DICTIONARIES

The Correct System for Memorizing Foreign Words

Acquiring vocabulary is one of the most important elements of learning a foreign language, because words allow us to express our thoughts, ask questions, and provide answers. An inadequate vocabulary can impede communication with a foreigner and make it difficult to understand a book or movie well.

The pace of activity in all spheres of modern life, including the learning of modern languages, has increased. Today, we need to memorize large amounts of information (grammar rules, foreign words, etc.) within a short period. However, this does not need to be difficult. All you need to do is to choose the right training materials, learn a few special techniques, and develop your individual training system.

Having a system is critical to the process of language learning. Many people fail to succeed in this regard; they cannot master a foreign language because they fail to follow a system comprised of selecting materials, organizing lessons, arranging new words to be learned, and so on. The lack of a system causes confusion and eventually, lowers self-confidence.

T&P Books' theme-based dictionaries can be included in the list of elements needed for creating an effective system for learning foreign words. These dictionaries were specially developed for learning purposes and are meant to help students effectively memorize words and expand their vocabulary.

Generally speaking, the process of learning words consists of three main elements:

- Reception (creation or acquisition) of a training material, such as a word list
- Work aimed at memorizing new words
- Work aimed at reviewing the learned words, such as self-testing

All three elements are equally important since they determine the quality of work and the final result. All three processes require certain skills and a well-thought-out approach.

New words are often encountered quite randomly when learning a foreign language and it may be difficult to include them all in a unified list. As a result, these words remain written on scraps of paper, in book margins, textbooks, and so on. In order to systematize such words, we have to create and continually update a "book of new words." A paper notebook, a netbook, or a tablet PC can be used for these purposes.

This "book of new words" will be your personal, unique list of words. However, it will only contain the words that you came across during the learning process. For example, you might have written down the words "Sunday," "Tuesday," and "Friday." However, there are additional words for days of the week, for example, "Saturday," that are missing, and your list of words would be incomplete. Using a theme dictionary, in addition to the "book of new words," is a reasonable solution to this problem.

The theme-based dictionary may serve as the basis for expanding your vocabulary.

It will be your big "book of new words" containing the most frequently used words of a foreign language already included. There are quite a few theme-based dictionaries available, and you should ensure that you make the right choice in order to get the maximum benefit from your purchase.

Therefore, we suggest using theme-based dictionaries from T&P Books Publishing as an aid to learning foreign words. Our books are specially developed for effective use in the sphere of vocabulary systematization, expansion and review.

Theme-based dictionaries are not a magical solution to learning new words. However, they can serve as your main database to aid foreign-language acquisition. Apart from theme dictionaries, you can have copybooks for writing down new words, flash cards, glossaries for various texts, as well as other resources; however, a good theme dictionary will always remain your primary collection of words.

T&P Books' theme-based dictionaries are specialty books that contain the most frequently used words in a language.

The main characteristic of such dictionaries is the division of words into themes. For example, the *City* theme contains the words "street," "crossroads," "square," "fountain," and so on. The *Talking* theme might contain words like "to talk," "to ask," "question," and "answer".

All the words in a theme are divided into smaller units, each comprising 3–5 words. Such an arrangement improves the perception of words and makes the learning process less tiresome. Each unit contains a selection of words with similar meanings or identical roots. This allows you to learn words in small groups and establish other associative links that have a positive effect on memorization.

The words on each page are placed in three columns: a word in your native language, its translation, and its transcription. Such positioning allows for the use of techniques for effective memorization. After closing the translation column, you can flip through and review foreign words, and vice versa. "This is an easy and convenient method of review – one that we recommend you do often."

Our theme-based dictionaries contain transcriptions for all the foreign words. Unfortunately, none of the existing transcriptions are able to convey the exact nuances of foreign pronunciation. That is why we recommend using the transcriptions only as a supplementary learning aid. Correct pronunciation can only be acquired with the help of sound. Therefore our collection includes audio theme-based dictionaries.

The process of learning words using T&P Books' theme-based dictionaries gives you the following advantages:

- You have correctly grouped source information, which predetermines your success at subsequent stages of word memorization

- Availability of words derived from the same root (lazy, lazily, lazybones), allowing you to memorize word units instead of separate words

- Small units of words facilitate the process of establishing associative links needed for consolidation of vocabulary

- You can estimate the number of learned words and hence your level of language knowledge

- The dictionary allows for the creation of an effective and high-quality revision process

- You can revise certain themes several times, modifying the revision methods and techniques

- Audio versions of the dictionaries help you to work out the pronunciation of words and develop your skills of auditory word perception

The T&P Books' theme-based dictionaries are offered in several variants differing in the number of words: 1.500, 3.000, 5.000, 7.000, and 9.000 words. There are also dictionaries containing 15,000 words for some language combinations. Your choice of dictionary will depend on your knowledge level and goals.

We sincerely believe that our dictionaries will become your trusty assistant in learning foreign languages and will allow you to easily acquire the necessary vocabulary.

TABLE OF CONTENTS

FAUNA 96

FLORA 103

COUNTRIES OF THE WORLD 107

PRONUNCIATION GUIDE

Letter	Swedish example	T&P phonetic alphabet	English example
Aa	bada	[a], [ɑː]	bath, to pass
Bb	tabell	[b]	baby, book
Cc [1]	licens	[s]	city, boss
Cc [2]	container	[k]	clock, kiss
Dd	andra	[d]	day, doctor
Ee	efter	[e]	elm, medal
Ff	flera	[f]	face, food
Gg [3]	gömma	[j]	yes, New York
Gg [4]	truga	[g]	game, gold
Hh	handla	[h]	home, have
Ii	tillhöra	[iː], [ɪ]	tree, big
Jj	jaga	[j]	yes, New York
Kk [5]	keramisk	[ɕ]	sheep, shop
Kk [6]	frisk	[k]	clock, kiss
Ll	tal	[l]	lace, people
Mm	medalj	[m]	magic, milk
Nn	panik	[n]	name, normal
Oo	tolv	[ɔ]	bottle, doctor
Pp	plommon	[p]	pencil, private
Qq	squash	[k]	clock, kiss
Rr	spelregler	[r]	rice, radio
Ss	spara	[s]	city, boss
Tt	tillhöra	[t]	tourist, trip
Uu	ungefär	[u], [ʉː]	soup, menu
Vv	overall	[v]	very, river
Ww [7]	kiwi	[w]	vase, winter
Xx	sax	[ks]	box, taxi
Yy	manikyr	[y], [yː]	fuel, tuna
Zz	zoolog	[s]	city, boss
Åå	sångare	[ə]	driver, teacher
Ää	tandläkare	[æ]	chess, man
Öö	kompositör	[ø]	eternal, church

Letter	Swedish example	T&P phonetic alphabet	English example

Combinations of letters

Ss [8]	sjösjuka	[ʃ]	machine, shark
sk [9]	skicka	[ʃ]	machine, shark
s [10]	först	[ʃ]	machine, shark
J j [11]	djärv	[j]	yes, New York
Lj [12]	ljus	[j]	yes, New York
kj, tj	kjol	[ɕ]	sheep, shop
ng	omkring	[ŋ]	English, ring

Comments

[*] kj pronouns as

[**] combination **ng** transfers a nasal sound

[1] before **e, i, y**

[2] elsewhere

[3] before **e, i, ä, ö**

[4] elsewhere

[5] before **e, i, ä, ö**

[6] elsewhere

[7] in loanwords

[8] in **sj, skj, stj**

[9] before stressed **e, i, y, ä, ö**

[10] in the combination **rs**

[11] in **dj, hj, gj, kj**

[12] at the beginning of words

ABBREVIATIONS
used in the vocabulary

English abbreviations

ab.	-	about
adj	-	adjective
adv	-	adverb
anim.	-	animate
as adj	-	attributive noun used as adjective
e.g.	-	for example
etc.	-	et cetera
fam.	-	familiar
fem.	-	feminine
form.	-	formal
inanim.	-	inanimate
masc.	-	masculine
math	-	mathematics
mil.	-	military
n	-	noun
pl	-	plural
pron.	-	pronoun
sb	-	somebody
sing.	-	singular
sth	-	something
v aux	-	auxiliary verb
vi	-	intransitive verb
vi, vt	-	intransitive, transitive verb
vt	-	transitive verb

Swedish abbreviations

pl	-	plural

Swedish articles

den	-	common gender
det	-	neuter
en	-	common gender
ett	-	neuter

BASIC CONCEPTS

1. Pronouns

I, me	**jag**	['ja:]
you	**du**	[dʉ:]
he	**han**	['han]
she	**hon**	['hʊn]
it	**det, den**	[dɛ], [dɛn]
we	**vi**	['vi]
you (to a group)	**ni**	['ni]
they	**de**	[de:]

2. Greetings. Salutations

Hello! (fam.)	**Hej!**	['hɛj]
Hello! (form.)	**Hej! Hallå!**	['hɛj], [ha'lʲo:]
Good morning!	**God morgon!**	[ˌgʊd 'mɔrgɔn]
Good afternoon!	**God dag!**	[ˌgʊd 'dag]
Good evening!	**God kväll!**	[ˌgʊd 'kvɛlʲ]
to say hello	**att hälsa**	[at 'hɛlʲsa]
Hi! (hello)	**Hej!**	['hɛj]
greeting (n)	**hälsning (en)**	['hɛlʲsniŋ]
to greet (vt)	**att hälsa**	[at 'hɛlʲsa]
How are you? (form.)	**Hur står det till?**	[hʉr sto: de 'tilʲ]
How are you? (fam.)	**Hur är det?**	[hʉr ɛr 'de:]
What's new?	**Vad är nytt?**	[vad æːr 'nʏt]
Goodbye! (form.)	**Adjö! Hej då!**	[a'jø:], [hɛj'do:]
Bye! (fam.)	**Hej då!**	[hɛj'do:]
See you soon!	**Vi ses!**	[vi ses]
Farewell!	**Adjö! Farväl!**	[a'jø:], [far'vɛ:lʲ]
to say goodbye	**att säga adjö**	[at 'sɛ:ja a'jø:]
So long!	**Hej då!**	[hɛj'do:]
Thank you!	**Tack!**	['tak]
Thank you very much!	**Tack så mycket!**	['tak sɔ 'mʏkə]
You're welcome	**Varsågod**	['va:ʂo:gʊd]
Don't mention it!	**Ingen orsak!**	['iŋən 'ʊ:ʂak]
It was nothing	**Ingen orsak!**	['iŋən 'ʊ:ʂak]
Excuse me! (fam.)	**Ursäkta, ...**	['ʉːˌʂɛkta ...]

| Excuse me! (form.) | Ursäkta mig, ... | ['ʉ:ˌsɛkta mɛj ...] |
| to excuse (forgive) | att ursäkta | [at 'ʉ:ˌsɛkta] |

to apologize (vi)	att ursäkta sig	[at 'ʉ:ˌsɛkta sɛj]
My apologies	Jag ber om ursäkt	[ja ber ɔm 'ʉ:ˌsɛkt]
I'm sorry!	Förlåt!	[fœ:'lʲo:t]
to forgive (vt)	att förlåta	[at 'fœ:ˌlʲo:ta]
It's okay! (that's all right)	Det gör inget	[dɛ jør 'iŋet]
please (adv)	snälla	['snɛla]

Don't forget!	Glöm inte!	['glʲø:m 'intə]
Certainly!	Naturligtvis!	[na'tʉrligvis]
Of course not!	Självklart inte!	['ɧɛlʲvklʲaṭ 'intə]
Okay! (I agree)	OK! Jag håller med.	[ɔ'kej] , [ja 'ho:lʲer me]
That's enough!	Det räcker!	[dɛ 'rɛkə]

3. Questions

Who?	Vem?	['vem]
What?	Vad?	['vad]
Where? (at, in)	Var?	['var]
Where (to)?	Vart?	['va:t]
From where?	Varifrån?	['varifro:n]
When?	När?	['næ:r]
Why? (What for?)	Varför?	['va:fø:r]
Why? (~ are you crying?)	Varför?	['va:fø:r]

What for?	För vad?	['før vad]
How? (in what way)	Hur?	['hʉ:r]
What? (What kind of ...?)	Vilken?	['vilʲkən]
Which?	Vilken?	['vilʲkən]

To whom?	Till vem?	[tilʲ 'vem]
About whom?	Om vem?	[ɔm 'vem]
About what?	Om vad?	[ɔm 'vad]
With whom?	Med vem?	[me 'vem]

How many?	Hur många?	[hʉr 'mɔŋa]
How much?	Hur mycket?	[hʉr 'mʏkə]
Whose?	Vems?	['vɛms]

4. Prepositions

with (accompanied by)	med	['me]
without	utan	['ʉtan]
to (indicating direction)	till	['tilʲ]
about (talking ~ ...)	om	['ɔm]
before (in time)	för, inför	['fø:r], ['infø:r]

in front of ...	framför	['framfø:r]
under (beneath, below)	under	['undər]
above (over)	över	['ø:vər]
on (atop)	på	[pɔ]
from (off, out of)	från	['frɔn]
of (made from)	av	[av]
in (e.g., ~ ten minutes)	om	['ɔm]
over (across the top of)	över	['ø:vər]

5. Function words. Adverbs. Part 1

Where? (at, in)	Var?	['var]
here (adv)	här	['hæ:r]
there (adv)	där	['dæ:r]
somewhere (to be)	någonstans	['nɔ:gɔn̩stans]
nowhere (not anywhere)	ingenstans	['iŋən̩stans]
by (near, beside)	vid	['vid]
by the window	vid fönstret	[vid 'fœnstrət]
Where (to)?	Vart?	['va:t]
here (e.g., come ~!)	hit	['hit]
there (e.g., to go ~)	dit	['dit]
from here (adv)	härifrån	['hæ:ri̩fro:n]
from there (adv)	därifrån	['dæ:ri̩fro:n]
close (adv)	nära	['næ:ra]
far (adv)	långt	['lʲɔŋt]
near (e.g., ~ Paris)	nära	['næ:ra]
nearby (adv)	i närheten	[i 'næ:r̩hetən]
not far (adv)	inte långt	['intə 'lʲɔŋt]
left (adj)	vänster	['vɛnstər]
on the left	till vänster	[tilʲ 'vɛnstər]
to the left	till vänster	[tilʲ 'vɛnstər]
right (adj)	höger	['hø:gər]
on the right	till höger	[tilʲ 'hø:gər]
to the right	till höger	[tilʲ 'hø:gər]
in front (adv)	framtill	['framtilʲ]
front (as adj)	främre	['frɛmrə]
ahead (the kids ran ~)	framåt	['framo:t]
behind (adv)	bakom, baktill	['bakɔm], ['bak'tilʲ]
from behind	bakifrån	['baki̩fro:n]
back (towards the rear)	tillbaka	[tilʲ'baka]

| middle | mitt (en) | ['mit] |
| in the middle | i mitten | [i 'mitən] |

at the side	från sidan	[frɔn 'sidan]
everywhere (adv)	överallt	['ø:vər‚alʲt]
around (in all directions)	runt omkring	[runt ɔm'kriŋ]

from inside	inifrån	['ini‚froːn]
somewhere (to go)	någonstans	['noːgɔn‚stans]
straight (directly)	rakt, rakt fram	['rakt], ['rakt fram]
back (e.g., come ~)	tillbaka	[tilʲ'baka]

| from anywhere | från var som helst | [frɔn va sɔm 'hɛlʲst] |
| from somewhere | från någonstans | [frɔn 'noːgɔn‚stans] |

firstly (adv)	för det första	['før de 'fœːʂta]
secondly (adv)	för det andra	['før de 'andra]
thirdly (adv)	för det tredje	['før de 'trɛdjə]

suddenly (adv)	plötsligt	['plʲøtslit]
at first (in the beginning)	i början	[i 'bœrjan]
for the first time	för första gången	['før 'fœːʂta 'gɔŋən]
long before ...	långt innan ...	['lʲɔŋt 'inan ...]
anew (over again)	på nytt	[pɔ 'nʏt]
for good (adv)	för gott	[før 'gɔt]

never (adv)	aldrig	['alʲdrig]
again (adv)	igen	['ijɛn]
now (adv)	nu	['nʉ:]
often (adv)	ofta	['ofta]
then (adv)	då	['do:]
urgently (quickly)	brådskande	['brɔ‚skandə]
usually (adv)	vanligtvis	['van‚litvis]

by the way, ...	förresten ...	[fœː'rɛstən ...]
possible (that is ~)	möjligen	['mœjligən]
probably (adv)	sannolikt	[sanʊ'likt]
maybe (adv)	kanske	['kanɧə]
besides ...	dessutom ...	[des'ʉːtʊm ...]
that's why ...	därför ...	['dæː:før ...]
in spite of ...	i trots av ...	[i 'trɔts av ...]
thanks to ...	tack vare ...	['tak ‚varə ...]

what (pron.)	vad	['vad]
that (conj.)	att	[at]
something	något	['noːgɔt]
anything (something)	något	['noːgɔt]
nothing	ingenting	['iŋəntiŋ]

who (pron.)	vem	['vem]
someone	någon	['noːgɔn]
somebody	någon	['noːgɔn]

nobody	ingen	['iŋən]
nowhere (a voyage to ~)	ingenstans	['iŋən͵stans]
nobody's	ingens	['iŋəns]
somebody's	någons	['noːgɔns]

so (I'm ~ glad)	så	['soː]
also (as well)	också	['ɔksoː]
too (as well)	också	['ɔksoː]

6. Function words. Adverbs. Part 2

Why?	Varför?	['vaːføːr]
for some reason	av någon anledning	[av 'noːgɔn 'an͵lˠedniŋ]
because ...	därför att ...	['dæːfør at ...]
for some purpose	av någon anledning	[av 'noːgɔn 'an͵lˠedniŋ]

and	och	['ɔ]
or	eller	['ɛlˠer]
but	men	['men]
for (e.g., ~ me)	för, till	['føːr]

too (~ many people)	för, alltför	['føːr], ['alˠtføːr]
only (exclusively)	bara, endast	['bara], ['ɛndast]
exactly (adv)	precis, exakt	[prɛ'sis], [ɛk'sakt]
about (more or less)	cirka	['sirka]

approximately (adv)	ungefär	['uŋə͵fæːr]
approximate (adj)	ungefärlig	['uŋə͵fæːʟig]
almost (adv)	nästan	['nɛstan]
the rest	rest (en)	['rɛst]

the other (second)	den andra	[dɛn 'andra]
other (different)	andre	['andrə]
each (adj)	var	['var]
any (no matter which)	vilken som helst	['vilˠkən sɔm 'hɛlˠst]
many, much (a lot of)	mycken, mycket	['mʏkən], ['mʏkə]
many people	många	['mɔŋa]
all (everyone)	alla	['alˠa]

in return for ...	i gengäld för ...	[i 'jɛŋɛld ͵før ...]
in exchange (adv)	i utbyte	[i 'ʉt͵bytə]
by hand (made)	för hand	[før 'hand]
hardly (negative opinion)	knappast	['knapast]

probably (adv)	sannolikt	[sanʋ'likt]
on purpose (intentionally)	med flit, avsiktligt	[me flit], ['avsiktlit]
by accident (adv)	tillfälligtvis	['tilˠfɔlitvis]

very (adv)	mycket	['mʏkə]
for example (adv)	till exempel	[tilˠ ɛk'sɛmpəl]

between	mellan	['mɛlʲan]
among	bland	['blʲand]
so much (such a lot)	så mycket	[sɔ 'mʏkə]
especially (adv)	särskilt	['sæːˌɕilʲt]

NUMBERS. MISCELLANEOUS

7. Cardinal numbers. Part 1

0 zero	noll	['nɔlʲ]
1 one	ett	[ɛt]
2 two	två	['tvoː]
3 three	tre	['treː]
4 four	fyra	['fyra]
5 five	fem	['fem]
6 six	sex	['sɛks]
7 seven	sju	['ɧʉː]
8 eight	åtta	['ota]
9 nine	nio	['niːʊ]
10 ten	tio	['tiːʊ]
11 eleven	elva	['ɛlʲva]
12 twelve	tolv	['tolʲv]
13 thirteen	tretton	['trɛtton]
14 fourteen	fjorton	['fjʊːʈon]
15 fifteen	femton	['fɛmton]
16 sixteen	sexton	['sɛkston]
17 seventeen	sjutton	['ɧʉːtton]
18 eighteen	arton	['aːʈon]
19 nineteen	nitton	['niːtton]
20 twenty	tjugo	['ɕʉgʊ]
21 twenty-one	tjugoett	['ɕʉgʊˌɛt]
22 twenty-two	tjugotvå	['ɕʉgʊˌtvoː]
23 twenty-three	tjugotre	['ɕʉgʊˌtreː]
30 thirty	trettio	['trɛttiʊ]
31 thirty-one	trettioett	['trɛttiʊˌɛt]
32 thirty-two	trettiotvå	['trɛttiʊˌtvoː]
33 thirty-three	trettiotre	['trɛttiʊˌtreː]
40 forty	fyrtio	['fœːʈiʊ]
41 forty-one	fyrtioett	['fœːʈiʊˌɛt]
42 forty-two	fyrtiotvå	['fœːʈiʊˌtvoː]
43 forty-three	fyrtiotre	['fœːʈiʊˌtreː]
50 fifty	femtio	['fɛmtiʊ]
51 fifty-one	femtioett	['fɛmtiʊˌɛt]
52 fifty-two	femtiotvå	['fɛmtiʊˌtvoː]

53 fifty-three	femtiotre	['fɛmtiʊˌtreː]
60 sixty	sextio	['sɛkstiʊ]
61 sixty-one	sextioett	['sɛkstiʊˌɛt]
62 sixty-two	sextiotvå	['sɛkstiʊˌtvoː]
63 sixty-three	sextiotre	['sɛkstiʊˌtreː]

70 seventy	sjuttio	['ɧuttiʊ]
71 seventy-one	sjuttioett	['ɧuttiʊˌɛt]
72 seventy-two	sjuttiotvå	['ɧuttiʊˌtvoː]
73 seventy-three	sjuttiotre	['ɧuttiʊˌtreː]

80 eighty	åttio	['ottiʊ]
81 eighty-one	åttioett	['ottiʊ'ɛt]
82 eighty-two	åttiotvå	['ottiʊˌtvoː]
83 eighty-three	åttiotre	['ottiʊˌtreː]

90 ninety	nittio	['nittiʊ]
91 ninety-one	nittioett	['nittiʊˌɛt]
92 ninety-two	nittiotvå	['nittiʊˌtvoː]
93 ninety-three	nittiotre	['nittiʊˌtreː]

8. Cardinal numbers. Part 2

100 one hundred	hundra (ett)	['hundra]
200 two hundred	tvåhundra	['tvoːˌhundra]
300 three hundred	trehundra	['treˌhundra]
400 four hundred	fyrahundra	['fyraˌhundra]
500 five hundred	femhundra	['femˌhundra]

600 six hundred	sexhundra	['sɛksˌhundra]
700 seven hundred	sjuhundra	['ɧʉːˌhundra]
800 eight hundred	åttahundra	['otaˌhundra]
900 nine hundred	niohundra	['niʊˌhundra]

1000 one thousand	tusen (ett)	['tʉːsən]
2000 two thousand	tvåtusen	['tvoːˌtʉːsən]
3000 three thousand	tretusen	['treˌtʉːsən]
10000 ten thousand	tiotusen	['tiːʊˌtʉːsən]
one hundred thousand	hundratusen	['hundraˌtʉːsən]
million	miljon (en)	[mi'ljʊn]
billion	miljard (en)	[mi'ljaːɖ]

9. Ordinal numbers

first (adj)	första	['fœːʂta]
second (adj)	andra	['andra]
third (adj)	tredje	['trɛdjə]
fourth (adj)	fjärde	['fjæːɖə]

fifth (adj)	**femte**	['fɛmtə]
sixth (adj)	**sjätte**	['ɧæːtə]
seventh (adj)	**sjunde**	['ɧundə]
eighth (adj)	**åttonde**	['ottɔndə]
ninth (adj)	**nionde**	['niːˌʊndə]
tenth (adj)	**tionde**	['tiːˌɔndə]

COLOURS. UNITS OF MEASUREMENT

10. Colors

color	**färg (en)**	['fæ:rj]
shade (tint)	**nyans (en)**	[ny'ans]
hue	**färgton (en)**	['fæ:rj͵tʊn]
rainbow	**regnbåge (en)**	['rɛgn͵bo:gə]
white (adj)	**vit**	['vit]
black (adj)	**svart**	['sva:t]
gray (adj)	**grå**	['gro:]
green (adj)	**grön**	['grø:n]
yellow (adj)	**gul**	['gʉ:lʲ]
red (adj)	**röd**	['rø:d]
blue (adj)	**blå**	['blʲo:]
light blue (adj)	**ljusblå**	['jʉ:s͵blʲo:]
pink (adj)	**rosa**	['rɔsa]
orange (adj)	**orange**	[ɔ'ranʃ]
violet (adj)	**violett**	[viʊ'lʲet]
brown (adj)	**brun**	['brʉ:n]
golden (adj)	**guld-**	['gulʲd-]
silvery (adj)	**silver-**	['silʲvər-]
beige (adj)	**beige**	['bɛʃ]
cream (adj)	**cremefärgad**	['krɛ:m͵fæ:rjad]
turquoise (adj)	**turkos**	[tur'ko:s]
cherry red (adj)	**körsbärsröd**	['çø:ʂbæ:ʂ͵rø:d]
lilac (adj)	**lila**	['lilʲa]
crimson (adj)	**karmosinröd**	[kar'mosin͵rø:d]
light (adj)	**ljus**	['jʉ:s]
dark (adj)	**mörk**	['mœ:rk]
bright, vivid (adj)	**klar**	['klʲar]
colored (pencils)	**färg-**	['fæ:rj-]
color (e.g., ~ film)	**färg-**	['fæ:rj-]
black-and-white (adj)	**svartvit**	['sva:t͵vit]
plain (one-colored)	**enfärgad**	['ɛn͵fæ:rjad]
multicolored (adj)	**mångfärgad**	['mɔŋ͵fæ:rjad]

11. Units of measurement

weight	vikt (en)	['vikt]
length	längd (en)	[ˈlɛŋd]
width	bredd (en)	['brɛd]
height	höjd (en)	['hœjd]
depth	djup (ett)	['jɯ:p]
volume	volym (en)	[vɔ'lʲym]
area	yta, areal (en)	['yta], [are'alʲ]
gram	gram (ett)	['gram]
milligram	milligram (ett)	['miliˌgram]
kilogram	kilogram (ett)	[ɕilʲɔ'gram]
ton	ton (en)	['tɯn]
pound	skålpund (ett)	['sko:lʲˌpund]
ounce	uns (ett)	['uns]
meter	meter (en)	['metər]
millimeter	millimeter (en)	['miliˌmetər]
centimeter	centimeter (en)	[sɛnti'metər]
kilometer	kilometer (en)	[ɕilʲɔ'metər]
mile	mil (en)	['milʲ]
inch	tum (en)	['tum]
foot	fot (en)	['fʊt]
yard	yard (en)	['ja:d]
square meter	kvadratmeter (en)	[kva'dratˌmetər]
hectare	hektar (ett)	[hɛk'tar]
liter	liter (en)	['litər]
degree	grad (en)	['grad]
volt	volt (en)	['vɔlʲt]
ampere	ampere (en)	[am'pɛr]
horsepower	hästkraft (en)	['hɛstˌkraft]
quantity	mängd, kvantitet (en)	['mɛŋt], [kwanti'tet]
a little bit of ...	få ..., inte många ...	['fo: ...], ['intə 'mɔŋa ...]
half	hälft (en)	['hɛlʲft]
dozen	dussin (ett)	['dusin]
piece (item)	stycke (ett)	['stʏkə]
size	storlek (en)	['stʊ:lʲek]
scale (map ~)	skala (en)	['skalʲa]
minimal (adj)	minimal	[mini'malʲ]
the smallest (adj)	minst	['minst]
medium (adj)	medel	['medəlʲ]
maximal (adj)	maximal	[maksi'malʲ]
the largest (adj)	störst	['stø:ʂt]

25

12. Containers

canning jar (glass ~)	glasburk (en)	['glʲasˌburk]
can	burk (en)	['burk]
bucket	hink (en)	['hiŋk]
barrel	tunna (en)	['tuna]

wash basin (e.g., plastic ~)	tvättfat (ett)	['tvætˌfat]
tank (100L water ~)	tank (en)	['taŋk]
hip flask	plunta, fickflaska (en)	['plʉnta], ['fikˌflʲaska]
jerrycan	dunk (en)	['duːŋk]
tank (e.g., tank car)	tank (en)	['taŋk]

mug	mugg (en)	['mug]
cup (of coffee, etc.)	kopp (en)	['kop]
saucer	tefat (ett)	['teˌfat]
glass (tumbler)	glas (ett)	['glʲas]
wine glass	vinglas (ett)	['vinˌglʲas]
stock pot (soup pot)	kastrull, gryta (en)	[ka'strulʲ], ['gryta]

bottle (~ of wine)	flaska (en)	['flʲaska]
neck (of the bottle, etc.)	flaskhals (en)	['flʲaskˌhalʲs]

carafe (decanter)	karaff (en)	[ka'raf]
pitcher	kanna (en) med handtag	['kana me 'hanˌtag]
vessel (container)	behållare (en)	[be'hoːʲˌlʲarə]
pot (crock, stoneware ~)	kruka (en)	['krʉka]
vase	vas (en)	['vas]

bottle (perfume ~)	flakong (en)	[flʲa'kɔŋ]
vial, small bottle	flaska (en)	['flʲaska]
tube (of toothpaste)	tub (en)	['tʉːb]

sack (bag)	säck (en)	['sɛk]
bag (paper ~, plastic ~)	påse (en)	['poːsə]
pack (of cigarettes, etc.)	paket (ett)	[pa'ket]

box (e.g., shoebox)	ask (en)	['ask]
crate	låda (en)	['lʲoːda]
basket	korg (en)	['kɔrj]

MAIN VERBS

13. The most important verbs. Part 1

to advise (vt)	att råda	[at 'ro:da]
to agree (say yes)	att samtycka	[at 'sam,tʏka]
to answer (vi, vt)	att svara	[at 'svara]
to apologize (vi)	att ursäkta sig	[at 'ʉ:,sɛkta sɛj]
to arrive (vi)	att ankomma	[at 'aŋ,kɔma]
to ask (~ oneself)	att fråga	[at 'fro:ga]
to ask (~ sb to do sth)	att be	[at 'be:]
to be (vi)	att vara	[at 'vara]
to be afraid	att frukta	[at 'frʉkta]
to be hungry	att vara hungrig	[at 'vara 'huŋrig]
to be interested in ...	att intressera sig	[at intrɛ'sera sɛj]
to be needed	att vara behövd	[at 'vara be'høːvd]
to be surprised	att bli förvånad	[at bli før'voːnad]
to be thirsty	att vara törstig	[at 'vara 'tø:ʂtig]
to begin (vt)	att begynna	[at be'jina]
to belong to ...	att tillhöra ...	[at 'tilˌhø:ra ...]
to boast (vi)	att skryta	[at 'skryta]
to break (split into pieces)	att bryta	[at 'bryta]
to call (~ for help)	att tillkalla	[at 'tilˌkalˡa]
can (v aux)	att kunna	[at 'kuna]
to catch (vt)	att fånga	[at 'fɔŋa]
to change (vt)	att ändra	[at 'ɛndra]
to choose (select)	att välja	[at 'vɛlja]
to come down (the stairs)	att gå ned	[at 'go: ˌned]
to compare (vt)	att jämföra	[at 'jɛmˌføra]
to complain (vi, vt)	att klaga	[at 'klˡaga]
to confuse (mix up)	att förväxla	[at før'vɛkslˡa]
to continue (vt)	att fortsätta	[at 'fʊtˌsæta]
to control (vt)	att kontrollera	[at kɔntrɔ'lˡera]
to cook (dinner)	att laga	[at 'lˡaga]
to cost (vt)	att kosta	[at 'kɔsta]
to count (add up)	att räkna	[at 'rɛkna]
to count on ...	att räkna med ...	[at 'rɛkna me ...]
to create (vt)	att skapa	[at 'skapa]
to cry (weep)	att gråta	[at 'gro:ta]

14. The most important verbs. Part 2

to deceive (vi, vt)	att fuska	[at 'fʉska]
to decorate (tree, street)	att pryda	[at 'pryda]
to defend (a country, etc.)	att försvara	[at fœ:'ʂvara]
to demand (request firmly)	att kräva	[at 'krɛ:va]
to dig (vt)	att gräva	[at 'grɛ:va]
to discuss (vt)	att diskutera	[at diskʉ'tera]
to do (vt)	att göra	[at 'jø:ra]
to doubt (have doubts)	att tvivla	[at 'tvivlʲa]
to drop (let fall)	att tappa	[at 'tapa]
to enter (room, house, etc.)	att komma in	[at 'kɔma 'in]
to excuse (forgive)	att ursäkta	[at 'ʉ:ˌʂɛkta]
to exist (vi)	att existera	[at ɛksi'stera]
to expect (foresee)	att förutse	[at 'førʉtˌsə]
to explain (vt)	att förklara	[at før'klʲara]
to fall (vi)	att falla	[at 'falʲa]
to find (vt)	att finna	[at 'fina]
to finish (vt)	att sluta	[at 'slʉ:ta]
to fly (vi)	att flyga	[at 'flʲyga]
to follow ... (come after)	att följa efter ...	[at 'følja 'ɛftər ...]
to forget (vi, vt)	att glömma	[at 'glʲœma]
to forgive (vt)	att förlåta	[at 'fœ:ˌlʲo:ta]
to give (vt)	att ge	[at je:]
to give a hint	att ge en vink	[at je: en 'viŋk]
to go (on foot)	att gå	[at 'go:]
to go for a swim	att bada	[at 'bada]
to go out (for dinner, etc.)	att gå ut	[at 'go: ʉt]
to guess (the answer)	att gissa	[at 'jisa]
to have (vt)	att ha	[at 'ha]
to have breakfast	att äta frukost	[at 'ɛ:ta 'frʉ:kɔst]
to have dinner	att äta kvällsmat	[at 'ɛ:ta 'kvɛlʲsˌmat]
to have lunch	att äta lunch	[at 'ɛ:ta ˌlʉnɕ]
to hear (vt)	att höra	[at 'hø:ra]
to help (vt)	att hjälpa	[at 'jɛlʲpa]
to hide (vt)	att gömma	[at 'jœma]
to hope (vi, vt)	att hoppas	[at 'hɔpas]
to hunt (vi, vt)	att jaga	[at 'jaga]
to hurry (vi)	att skynda sig	[at 'ɧynda sɛj]

15. The most important verbs. Part 3

to inform (vt)	att informera	[at infɔr'mera]
to insist (vi, vt)	att insistera	[at insi'stera]
to insult (vt)	att förolämpa	[at 'førʊˌlʲɛmpa]
to invite (vt)	att inbjuda, att invitera	[at in'bjʉ:da], [at invi'tera]
to joke (vi)	att skämta, att skoja	[at 'ʃɛmta], [at 'skɔja]

to keep (vt)	att behålla	[at be'hɔːlʲa]
to keep silent	att tiga	[at 'tiga]
to kill (vt)	att döda, att mörda	[at 'dø:da], [at 'mø:ɖa]
to know (sb)	att känna	[at 'ɕɛna]
to know (sth)	att veta	[at 'veta]
to laugh (vi)	att skratta	[at 'skrata]

to liberate (city, etc.)	att befria	[at be'fria]
to like (I like ...)	att gilla	[at 'jilʲa]
to look for ... (search)	att söka ...	[at 'sø:ka ...]
to love (sb)	att älska	[at 'ɛlʲska]
to make a mistake	att göra fel	[at 'jø:ra ˌfelʲ]
to manage, to run	att styra, att leda	[at 'styra], [at 'lʲeda]
to mean (signify)	att betyda	[at be'tyda]
to mention (talk about)	att omnämna	[at 'ɔmˌnɛmna]
to miss (school, etc.)	att missa	[at 'misa]
to notice (see)	att märka	[at 'mæ:rka]

to object (vi, vt)	att invända	[at 'inˌvɛnda]
to observe (see)	att observera	[at ɔbsɛr'vera]
to open (vt)	att öppna	[at 'øpna]
to order (meal, etc.)	att beställa	[at be'stɛlʲa]
to order (mil.)	att beordra	[at be'o:ɖra]
to own (possess)	att besitta, att äga	[at be'sita], [at 'ɛ:ga]
to participate (vi)	att delta	[at 'dɛlʲta]
to pay (vi, vt)	att betala	[at be'talʲa]
to permit (vt)	att tillåta	[at 'tilʲo:ta]
to plan (vt)	att planera	[at plʲa'nera]
to play (children)	att leka	[at 'lʲeka]

to pray (vi, vt)	att be	[at 'be:]
to prefer (vt)	att föredra	[at 'førədra]
to promise (vt)	att lova	[at 'lʲova]
to pronounce (vt)	att uttala	[at 'ʉtˌtalʲa]
to propose (vt)	att föreslå	[at 'førəˌslʲo:]
to punish (vt)	att straffa	[at 'strafa]

16. The most important verbs. Part 4

to read (vi, vt)	att läsa	[at 'lʲɛ:sa]
to recommend (vt)	att rekommendera	[at rekɔmən'dera]

to refuse (vi, vt)	att vägra	[at 'vɛgra]
to regret (be sorry)	att beklaga	[at be'klʲaga]
to rent (sth from sb)	att hyra	[at 'hyra]
to repeat (say again)	att upprepa	[at 'uprepa]
to reserve, to book	att reservera	[at resɛr'vera]
to run (vi)	att löpa, att springa	[at 'lʲø:pa], [at 'spriŋa]
to save (rescue)	att rädda	[at 'rɛda]
to say (~ thank you)	att säga	[at 'sɛ:ja]
to scold (vt)	att skälla	[at 'ɧɛlʲa]
to see (vt)	att se	[at 'se:]
to sell (vt)	att sälja	[at 'sɛlja]
to send (vt)	att skicka	[at 'ɧika]
to shoot (vi)	att skjuta	[at 'ɧʉ:ta]
to shout (vi)	att skrika	[at 'skrika]
to show (vt)	att visa	[at 'visa]
to sign (document)	att underteckna	[at 'undə͵tɛkna]
to sit down (vi)	att sätta sig	[at 'sæta sɛj]
to smile (vi)	att småle	[at 'smo:lʲe]
to speak (vi, vt)	att tala	[at 'talʲa]
to steal (money, etc.)	att stjäla	[at 'ɧɛ:lʲa]
to stop (for pause, etc.)	att stanna	[at 'stana]
to stop	att sluta	[at 'slʉ:ta]
(please ~ calling me)		
to study (vt)	att studera	[at stu'dera]
to swim (vi)	att simma	[at 'sima]
to take (vt)	att ta	[at ta]
to think (vi, vt)	att tänka	[at 'tɛŋka]
to threaten (vt)	att hota	[at 'huta]
to touch (with hands)	att röra	[at 'rø:ra]
to translate (vt)	att översätta	[at 'ø:və͵sæta]
to trust (vt)	att lita på	[at 'lita pɔ]
to try (attempt)	att pröva	[at 'prø:va]
to turn (e.g., ~ left)	att svänga	[at 'svɛŋa]
to underestimate (vt)	att underskatta	[at 'undə͵skata]
to understand (vt)	att förstå	[at fœ:'ʂto:]
to unite (vt)	att förena	[at 'førena]
to wait (vt)	att vänta	[at 'vɛnta]
to want (wish, desire)	att vilja	[at 'vilja]
to warn (vt)	att varna	[at 'va:ŋa]
to work (vi)	att arbeta	[at 'ar͵beta]
to write (vt)	att skriva	[at 'skriva]
to write down	att skriva ner	[at 'skriva ner]

TIME. CALENDAR

17. Weekdays

Monday	**måndag (en)**	['mɔn,dag]
Tuesday	**tisdag (en)**	['tis,dag]
Wednesday	**onsdag (en)**	['ʊns,dag]
Thursday	**torsdag (en)**	['tʊːʂ,dag]
Friday	**fredag (en)**	['fre,dag]
Saturday	**lördag (en)**	['lˈøːdag]
Sunday	**söndag (en)**	['sœn,dag]

today (adv)	**i dag**	[i 'dag]
tomorrow (adv)	**i morgon**	[i 'mɔrgɔn]
the day after tomorrow	**i övermorgon**	[i 'øːvə,mɔrgɔn]
yesterday (adv)	**i går**	[i 'goːr]
the day before yesterday	**i förrgår**	[i 'fœːr,goːr]

day	**dag (en)**	['dag]
working day	**arbetsdag (en)**	['arbets,dag]
public holiday	**helgdag (en)**	['hɛlj,dag]
day off	**ledig dag (en)**	['lˈedig ,dag]
weekend	**helg, veckohelg (en)**	[hɛlj], ['vɛkɔ,hɛlj]

all day long	**hela dagen**	['helˈa 'dagən]
the next day (adv)	**nästa dag**	['nɛsta ,dag]
two days ago	**för två dagar sedan**	[før ,tvoː 'dagar 'sedan]
the day before	**dagen innan**	['dagən 'inan]
daily (adj)	**daglig**	['daglig]
every day (adv)	**varje dag**	['varjə dag]

week	**vecka (en)**	['vɛka]
last week (adv)	**förra veckan**	['fœːra 'vɛkan]
next week (adv)	**i nästa vecka**	[i 'nɛsta 'vɛka]
weekly (adj)	**vecko-**	['vɛkɔ-]
every week (adv)	**varje vecka**	['varjə 'vɛka]
twice a week	**två gångar i veckan**	[tvoː 'gɔŋar i 'vɛkan]
every Tuesday	**varje tisdag**	['varjə ,tisdag]

18. Hours. Day and night

morning	**morgon (en)**	['mɔrgɔn]
in the morning	**på morgonen**	[pɔ 'mɔrgɔnən]
noon, midday	**middag (en)**	['mid,dag]

in the afternoon	på eftermiddagen	[pɔ 'ɛftə‚midagən]
evening	kväll (en)	[kvɛlʲ]
in the evening	på kvällen	[pɔ 'kvɛlʲen]
night	natt (en)	['nat]
at night	om natten	[ɔm 'natən]
midnight	midnatt (en)	['mid‚nat]

second	sekund (en)	[se'kund]
minute	minut (en)	[mi'nʉːt]
hour	timme (en)	['timə]
half an hour	halvtimme (en)	['halʲv‚timə]
a quarter-hour	kvart (en)	['kvaːt]
fifteen minutes	femton minuter	['fɛmtɔn mi'nʉːtər]
24 hours	dygn (ett)	['dʏgn]

sunrise	soluppgång (en)	['sʊlʲ ‚up'gɔŋ]
dawn	gryning (en)	['gryniŋ]
early morning	tidig morgon (en)	['tidig 'mɔrgɔn]
sunset	solnedgång (en)	['sʊlʲ 'ned‚gɔŋ]

early in the morning	tidigt på morgonen	['tidit pɔ 'mɔrgɔnən]
this morning	i morse	[i 'mɔːʂə]
tomorrow morning	i morgon bitti	[i 'mɔrgɔn 'biti]

this afternoon	i eftermiddag	[i 'ɛftə‚midag]
in the afternoon	på eftermiddagen	[pɔ 'ɛftə‚midagən]
tomorrow afternoon	i morgon eftermiddag	[i 'mɔrgɔn 'ɛftə‚midag]

| tonight (this evening) | i kväll | [i 'kvɛlʲ] |
| tomorrow night | i morgon kväll | [i 'mɔrgɔn 'kvɛlʲ] |

at 3 o'clock sharp	precis klockan tre	[prɛ'sis 'klʲɔkan treː]
about 4 o'clock	vid fyratiden	[vid 'fyra‚tidən]
by 12 o'clock	vid klockan tolv	[vid 'klʲɔkan 'tɔlʲv]

in 20 minutes	om tjugo minuter	[ɔm 'ɕʉgɔ mi'nʉːtər]
in an hour	om en timme	[ɔm en 'timə]
on time (adv)	i tid	[i 'tid]

a quarter of ...	kvart i ...	['kvaːʈ i ...]
within an hour	inom en timme	['inɔm en 'timə]
every 15 minutes	varje kvart	['varjə kvaːʈ]
round the clock	dygnet runt	['dʏgnet ‚runt]

19. Months. Seasons

January	januari	['janu‚ari]
February	februari	[fɛbrʉ'ari]
March	mars	['maːʂ]
April	april	[a'prilʲ]

| May | maj | ['maj] |
| June | juni | ['juːni] |

July	juli	['juːli]
August	augusti	[au'gusti]
September	september	[sɛp'tɛmbər]
October	oktober	[ɔk'tʊbər]
November	november	[nɔ'vɛmbər]
December	december	[de'sɛmbər]

spring	vår (en)	['voːr]
in spring	på våren	[pɔ 'voːrən]
spring (as adj)	vår-	['voːr-]

summer	sommar (en)	['sɔmar]
in summer	på sommaren	[pɔ 'sɔmarən]
summer (as adj)	sommar-	['sɔmar-]

fall	höst (en)	['høst]
in fall	på hösten	[pɔ 'høstən]
fall (as adj)	höst-	['høst-]

winter	vinter (en)	['vintər]
in winter	på vintern	[pɔ 'vintərn]
winter (as adj)	vinter-	['vintər-]

month	månad (en)	['moːnad]
this month	den här månaden	[dɛn hæːr 'moːnadən]
next month	nästa månad	['nɛsta 'moːnad]
last month	förra månaden	['fœːra 'moːnadən]

a month ago	för en månad sedan	['før en 'moːnad 'sedan]
in a month (a month later)	om en månad	[ɔm en 'moːnad]
in 2 months (2 months later)	om två månader	[ɔm tvoː 'moːnadər]
the whole month	en hel månad	[en helʲ 'moːnad]
all month long	hela månaden	['helʲa 'moːnadən]

monthly (~ magazine)	månatlig	[mo'natlig]
monthly (adv)	månatligen	[mo'natligən]
every month	varje månad	['varjə ˌmoːnad]
twice a month	två gånger i månaden	[tvoː 'gɔŋər i 'mɔːnadən]

year	år (ett)	['oːr]
this year	i år	[i 'oːr]
next year	nästa år	['nɛsta ˌoːr]
last year	i fjol, förra året	[i 'fjʊlʲ], ['fœːra 'oːret]

a year ago	för ett år sedan	['før et 'oːr 'sedan]
in a year	om ett år	[ɔm et 'oːr]
in two years	om två år	[ɔm tvoː 'oːr]
the whole year	ett helt år	[ɛt helʲt 'oːr]

all year long	hela året	['hel'a 'o:ret]
every year	varje år	['varjə 'o:r]
annual (adj)	årlig	['o:lig]
annually (adv)	årligen	['o:ligən]
4 times a year	fyra gånger om året	['fyra 'goŋər ɔm 'o:ret]

date (e.g., today's ~)	datum (ett)	['datum]
date (e.g., ~ of birth)	datum (ett)	['datum]
calendar	almanacka (en)	['al'manaka]

half a year	halvår (ett)	['hal'v‚o:r]
six months	halvår (ett)	['hal'v‚o:r]
season (summer, etc.)	årstid (en)	['o:ʂ‚tid]
century	sekel (ett)	['sekəl']

TRAVEL. HOTEL

20. Trip. Travel

tourism, travel	turism (en)	[tuˈrism]
tourist	turist (en)	[tuˈrist]
trip, voyage	resa (en)	[ˈresa]
adventure	äventyr (ett)	[ˈɛːvɛnˌtyr]
trip, journey	tripp (en)	[ˈtrip]
vacation	semester (en)	[seˈmɛstər]
to be on vacation	att ha semester	[at ha seˈmɛstər]
rest	uppehåll (ett), vila (en)	[ˈupəˈhoːlⁱ], [ˈvilⁱa]
train	tåg (ett)	[ˈtoːg]
by train	med tåg	[me ˈtoːg]
airplane	flygplan (ett)	[ˈflⁱygplⁱan]
by airplane	med flygplan	[me ˈflⁱygplⁱan]
by car	med bil	[me ˈbilⁱ]
by ship	med båt	[me ˈboːt]
luggage	bagage (ett)	[baˈgaːʃ]
suitcase	resväska (en)	[ˈrɛsˌvɛska]
luggage cart	bagagevagn (en)	[baˈgaːʃˌvagn]
passport	pass (ett)	[ˈpas]
visa	visum (ett)	[ˈviːsum]
ticket	biljett (en)	[biˈlⁱet]
air ticket	flygbiljett (en)	[ˈflⁱyg biˌlⁱet]
guidebook	reseguidebok (en)	[ˈreseˌgajdbʊk]
map (tourist ~)	karta (en)	[ˈkaːʈa]
area (rural ~)	område (ett)	[ˈɔmˌroːdə]
place, site	plats (en)	[ˈplⁱats]
exotica (n)	(det) exotiska	[ɛˈksɔtiska]
exotic (adj)	exotisk	[ɛkˈsɔtisk]
amazing (adj)	förunderlig	[føˈrundelig]
group	grupp (en)	[ˈgrup]
excursion, sightseeing tour	utflykt (en)	[ˈʉtˌflⁱykt]
guide (person)	guide (en)	[ˈgajd]

21. Hotel

hotel	hotell (ett)	[hʊ'tɛlʲ]
motel	motell (ett)	[mʊ'tɛlʲ]
three-star (~ hotel)	trestjärnigt	['tre͵ɧæːɳit]
five-star	femstjärnigt	[fɛm͵ɧæːɳit]
to stay (in a hotel, etc.)	att bo	[at 'bʊː]
room	rum (ett)	['ruːm]
single room	enkelrum (ett)	['ɛŋkəlʲ͵ruːm]
double room	dubbelrum (ett)	['dubəlʲ͵ruːm]
to book a room	att boka rum	[at 'bʊka 'ruːm]
half board	halvpension (en)	['halʲv͵pan'ɧʊn]
full board	helpension (en)	['helʲ͵pan'ɧʊn]
with bath	med badkar	[me 'bad͵kar]
with shower	med dusch	[me 'duʃ]
satellite television	satellit-TV (en)	[satɛ'liːt 'teve]
air-conditioner	luftkonditionerare (en)	['lʉft͵kɔndiɧʊ'nerarə]
towel	handduk (en)	['hand͵dʉːk]
key	nyckel (en)	['nʏkəlʲ]
administrator	administratör (en)	[administra'tør]
chambermaid	städerska (en)	['stɛːdɛʂka]
porter, bellboy	bärare (en)	['bæːrarə]
doorman	portier (en)	[pɔː'ʈeː]
restaurant	restaurang (en)	[rɛstɔ'raŋ]
pub, bar	bar (en)	['bar]
breakfast	frukost (en)	['frʉːkɔst]
dinner	kvällsmat (en)	['kvɛlʲs͵mat]
buffet	buffet (en)	[bu'fet]
lobby	lobby (en)	['lʲɔbi]
elevator	hiss (en)	['his]
DO NOT DISTURB	STÖR EJ!	['støːr ɛj]
NO SMOKING	RÖKNING FÖRBJUDEN	['rœkniŋ førbjʉːdən]

22. Sightseeing

monument	monument (ett)	[mɔnu'mɛnt]
fortress	fästning (en)	['fɛstniŋ]
palace	palats (ett)	[pa'lʲats]
castle	borg (en)	['bɔrj]
tower	torn (ett)	['tʊːɳ]
mausoleum	mausoleum (ett)	[maʊsʊ'lʲeum]

architecture	arkitektur (en)	[arkitɛk'tʉːr]
medieval (adj)	medeltida	['medəlˌtida]
ancient (adj)	gammal	['gamalʲ]
national (adj)	nationell	[natɧʊ'nɛlʲ]
famous (monument, etc.)	berömd	[be'rœmd]

tourist	turist (en)	[tu'rist]
guide (person)	guide (en)	['gajd]
excursion, sightseeing tour	utflykt (en)	['ʉtˌflʲykt]
to show (vt)	att visa	[at 'visa]
to tell (vt)	att berätta	[at be'ræta]

to find (vt)	att hitta	[at 'hita]
to get lost (lose one's way)	att gå vilse	[at 'goː 'vilʲsə]
map (e.g., subway ~)	karta (en)	['kaːʈa]
map (e.g., city ~)	karta (en)	['kaːʈa]

souvenir, gift	souvenir (en)	[suvɛ'niːr]
gift shop	souvenirbutik (en)	[suvɛ'niːr bu'tik]
to take pictures	att fotografera	[at fʊtʊgra'fera]
to have one's picture taken	att bli fotograferad	[at bli fʊtʊgra'ferad]

TRANSPORTATION

23. Airport

airport	**flygplats (en)**	['fly̥g,plʲaʦ]
airplane	**flygplan (ett)**	['fly̥gplʲan]
airline	**flygbolag (ett)**	['fly̥g,bʊlʲag]
air traffic controller	**flygledare (en)**	['fly̥g,lʲedarə]
departure	**avgång (en)**	['av,gɔŋ]
arrival	**ankomst (en)**	['aŋ,kɔmst]
to arrive (by plane)	**att ankomma**	[at 'aŋ,kɔma]
departure time	**avgångstid (en)**	['avgɔŋs,tid]
arrival time	**ankomsttid (en)**	['aŋkɔmst,tid]
to be delayed	**att bli försenad**	[at bli fœ:'ʂɛnad]
flight delay	**avgångsförsening (en)**	['avgɔŋs,fœ:'ʂɛniŋ]
information board	**informationstavla (en)**	[infɔrma'ɧʊns,tavlʲa]
information	**information (en)**	[infɔrma'ɧʊn]
to announce (vt)	**att meddela**	[at 'me,delʲa]
flight (e.g., next ~)	**flyg (ett)**	['fly̥g]
customs	**tull (en)**	['tulʲ]
customs officer	**tulltjänsteman (en)**	['tulʲ 'ɕɛnstə,man]
customs declaration	**tulldeklaration (en)**	['tulʲ,dɛklʲara'ɧʊn]
to fill out (vt)	**att fylla i**	[at 'fylʲa 'i]
to fill out the declaration	**att fylla i en tulldeklaration**	[at 'fylʲa i en 'tulʲ,dɛklʲara'ɧʊn]
passport control	**passkontroll (en)**	['paskɔn,trolʲ]
luggage	**bagage (ett)**	[ba'ga:ʃ]
hand luggage	**handbagage (ett)**	['hand ba,ga:ʃ]
luggage cart	**bagagevagn (en)**	[ba'ga:ʃ ,vagn]
landing	**landning (en)**	['lʲandniŋ]
landing strip	**landningsbana (en)**	['lʲandniŋs,bana]
to land (vi)	**att landa**	[at 'lʲanda]
airstairs	**trappa (en)**	['trapa]
check-in	**incheckning (en)**	['in,ɕɛkniŋ]
check-in counter	**incheckningsdisk (en)**	['in,ɕɛkniŋs 'disk]
to check-in (vi)	**att checka in**	[at 'ɕɛka in]
boarding pass	**boardingkort (ett)**	['bɔ:dịŋ,kɔ:t]

departure gate	gate (en)	['gejt]
transit	transit (en)	['transit]
to wait (vt)	att vänta	[at 'vɛnta]
departure lounge	väntsal (en)	['vɛntˌsalʲ]
to see off	att vinka av	[at 'viŋka av]
to say goodbye	att säga adjö	[at 'sɛ:ja a'jø:]

24. Airplane

airplane	flygplan (ett)	['flʲygplʲan]
air ticket	flygbiljett (en)	['flʲyg biˌlʲet]
airline	flygbolag (ett)	['flʲygˌbʊlʲag]
airport	flygplats (en)	['flʲygˌplʲats]
supersonic (adj)	överljuds-	['ø:vərjʉ:ds-]

captain	kapten (en)	[kap'ten]
crew	besättning (en)	[be'sætniŋ]
pilot	pilot (en)	[pi'lʲʊt]
flight attendant (fem.)	flygvärdinna (en)	['flʲygˌvæ:dina]
navigator	styrman (en)	['styrˌman]

wings	vingar (pl)	['viŋar]
tail	stjärtfena (en)	['ɧæ:t fe:na]
cockpit	cockpit, förarkabin (en)	['kɔkpit], ['fø:rarˌka'bin]
engine	motor (en)	['mʊtʊr]
undercarriage (landing gear)	landningsställ (ett)	['landniŋsˌstɛlʲ]
turbine	turbin (en)	[tur'bin]

propeller	propeller (en)	[prʊ'pɛlʲər]
black box	svart låda (en)	['sva:ʈ 'lʲo:da]
yoke (control column)	styrspak (ett)	['sty:ˌspak]
fuel	bränsle (ett)	['brɛnslʲe]

safety card	säkerhetsinstruktion (en)	['sɛ:kərhets instruk'ɧʊn]
oxygen mask	syremask (en)	['syreˌmask]
uniform	uniform (en)	[uni'fɔrm]
life vest	räddningsväst (en)	['rɛdniŋˌvɛst]
parachute	fallskärm (en)	['falʲˌɧæ:rm]

takeoff	start (en)	['sta:t]
to take off (vi)	att lyfta	[at 'lʲyfta]
runway	startbana (en)	['sta:ʈˌba:na]

visibility	siktbarhet (en)	['siktbarˌhet]
flight (act of flying)	flygning (en)	['flʲygniŋ]
altitude	höjd (en)	['hœjd]
air pocket	luftgrop (en)	['lʉftˌgrʊp]
seat	plats (en)	['plʲats]
headphones	hörlurar (pl)	['hœ:ˌlʲʉ:rar]

folding tray (tray table)	utfällbart bord (ett)	['ɵtfɛlʲ‚bart 'bʊːd]
airplane window	fönster (ett)	['fœnstər]
aisle	mittgång (en)	['mit‚gɔŋ]

25. Train

train	tåg (ett)	['toːg]
commuter train	lokaltåg, pendeltåg (ett)	[lʲoʹkalʲ‚toːg], ['pendəl‚toːg],
express train	expresståg (ett)	[ɛksʹprɛs‚toːg]
diesel locomotive	diesellokomotiv (ett)	['disəlʲ lʲokɔmɔ'tiv]
steam locomotive	ånglokomotiv (en)	['ɔŋ‚lʲokɔmɔ'tiv]
passenger car	vagn (en)	['vagn]
dining car	restaurangvagn (en)	[rɛstɔ'raŋ‚vagn]
rails	räls, rälsar (pl)	['rɛlʲs], ['rɛlʲsar]
railroad	järnväg (en)	['jæːn‚vɛːg]
railway tie	sliper (en)	['slipər]
platform (railway ~)	perrong (en)	[pɛ'rɔŋ]
track (~ 1, 2, etc.)	spår (ett)	['spoːr]
semaphore	semafor (en)	[sema'fɔr]
station	station (en)	[sta'ɧʊn]
engineer (train driver)	lokförare (en)	['lʲʊk‚føːrarə]
porter (of luggage)	bärare (en)	['bæːrarə]
car attendant	tågvärd (en)	['toːg‚væːd]
passenger	passagerare (en)	[pasa'ɧerarə]
conductor	kontrollant (en)	[kontrɔ'lʲant]
(ticket inspector)		
corridor (in train)	korridor (en)	[kɔri'dɔːr]
emergency brake	nödbroms (en)	['nøːd‚brɔms]
compartment	kupé (en)	[kʉ'peː]
berth	slaf, säng (en)	['slaf], ['sɛŋ]
upper berth	överslaf (en)	['øvə‚slaf]
lower berth	underslaf (en)	['undə‚slaf]
bed linen, bedding	sängkläder (pl)	['sɛŋ‚klʲɛːdər]
ticket	biljett (en)	[bi'lʲet]
schedule	tidtabell (en)	['tid ta'bɛlʲ]
information display	informationstavla (en)	[infɔrma'ɧʊns‚tavlʲa]
to leave, to depart	att avgå	[at 'av‚goː]
departure (of train)	avgång (en)	['av‚gɔŋ]
to arrive (ab. train)	att ankomma	[at 'aŋ‚koma]
arrival	ankomst (en)	['aŋ‚komst]
to arrive by train	att ankomma med tåget	[at 'aŋ‚koma me 'toːgət]
to get on the train	att stiga på tåget	[at 'stiga pɔ 'toːgət]

to get off the train	att stiga av tåget	[at 'stiga av 'to:gət]
train wreck	tågolycka (en)	['to:g ʊ:'lʲyka]
to derail (vi)	att spåra ur	[at 'spo:ra ɐ:r]
steam locomotive	ånglokomotiv (en)	['ɔŋˌlʲɔkɔmɔ'tiv]
stoker, fireman	eldare (en)	['ɛlʲdarə]
firebox	eldstad (en)	['ɛlʲdˌstad]
coal	kol (ett)	['kɔlʲ]

26. Ship

ship	skepp (ett)	['ɧɛp]
vessel	fartyg (ett)	['fa:ˌtyg]
steamship	ångbåt (en)	['ɔŋˌbo:t]
riverboat	flodbåt (en)	['flʲʊdˌbo:t]
cruise ship	kryssningfartyg (ett)	['krysniŋˌfa:'tyg]
cruiser	kryssare (en)	['krʏsarə]
yacht	jakt (en)	['jakt]
tugboat	bogserbåt (en)	['bʊksɛ:rˌbo:t]
barge	pråm (en)	['pro:m]
ferry	färja (en)	['fæ:rja]
sailing ship	segelbåt (en)	['segəlʲˌbo:t]
brigantine	brigantin (en)	[brigan'tin]
ice breaker	isbrytare (en)	['isˌbrytarə]
submarine	ubåt (en)	[ɐ:'bo:t]
boat (flat-bottomed ~)	båt (en)	['bo:t]
dinghy	jolle (en)	['jɔlʲe]
lifeboat	livbåt (en)	['livˌbo:t]
motorboat	motorbåt (en)	['mʊtʊrˌbo:t]
captain	kapten (en)	[kap'ten]
seaman	matros (en)	[ma'trʊs]
sailor	sjöman (en)	['ɧø:ˌman]
crew	besättning (en)	[be'sætniŋ]
boatswain	båtsman (en)	['bɔtsman]
ship's boy	jungman (en)	['jɵŋˌman]
cook	kock (en)	['kɔk]
ship's doctor	skeppsläkare (en)	['ɧɛpˌlʲɛ:karə]
deck	däck (ett)	['dɛk]
mast	mast (en)	['mast]
sail	segel (ett)	['segəlʲ]
hold	lastrum (ett)	['lʲastˌrʊ:m]
bow (prow)	bog (en)	['bʊg]

stern	akter (en)	['aktər]
oar	åra (en)	['oːra]
screw propeller	propeller (en)	[prʊ'pɛlʲər]

cabin	hytt (en)	['hʏt]
wardroom	officersmäss (en)	[ɔfi'seːrsˌmɛs]
engine room	maskinrum (ett)	[ma'ɧiːnˌruːm]
bridge	kommandobrygga (en)	[kɔm'andʊˌbrʏga]
radio room	radiohytt (en)	['radiʊˌhʏt]
wave (radio)	våg (en)	['voːg]
logbook	loggbok (en)	['lʲɔgˌbʊk]

spyglass	tubkikare (en)	['tʊbˌɕikarə]
bell	klocka (en)	['klʲɔka]
flag	flagga (en)	['flʲaga]

| hawser (mooring ~) | tross (en) | ['trɔs] |
| knot (bowline, etc.) | knop, knut (en) | ['knʊp], ['knʊt] |

| deckrails | räcken (pl) | ['rɛkən] |
| gangway | landgång (en) | ['lʲandˌgɔŋ] |

anchor	ankar (ett)	['aŋkar]
to weigh anchor	att lätta ankar	[at 'lʲæta 'aŋkar]
to drop anchor	att kasta ankar	[at 'kasta 'aŋkar]
anchor chain	ankarkätting (en)	['aŋkarˌɕætiŋ]

port (harbor)	hamn (en)	['hamn]
quay, wharf	kaj (en)	['kaj]
to berth (moor)	att förtöja	[at fœː'tɶːja]
to cast off	att kasta loss	[at 'kasta 'lʲɔs]

trip, voyage	resa (en)	['resa]
cruise (sea trip)	kryssning (en)	['krʏsniŋ]
course (route)	kurs (en)	['kuːʂ]
route (itinerary)	rutt (en)	['rut]

fairway	farled, segelled (en)	['faːʎed], ['segəlˌled]
(safe water channel)		
shallows	grund (ett)	['grʊnd]
to run aground	att gå på grund	[at 'goː pɔ 'grʊnd]

storm	storm (en)	['stɔrm]
signal	signal (en)	[sig'nalʲ]
to sink (vi)	att sjunka	[at 'ɧuŋka]
Man overboard!	Man överbord!	['man 'øːvəˌbuːɖ]
SOS (distress signal)	SOS	[ɛso'ɛs]
ring buoy	livboj (en)	['livˌbɔj]

CITY

27. Urban transportation

bus	buss (en)	['bus]
streetcar	spårvagn (en)	['spo:r‚vagn]
trolley bus	trådbuss (en)	['tro:d‚bus]
route (of bus, etc.)	rutt (en)	['rut]
number (e.g., bus ~)	nummer (ett)	['numər]
to go by ...	att åka med ...	[at 'o:ka me ...]
to get on (~ the bus)	att stiga på ...	[at 'stiga pɔ ...]
to get off ...	att stiga av ...	[at 'stiga 'av ...]
stop (e.g., bus ~)	hållplats (en)	['hɔ:lʲ‚plats]
next stop	nästa hållplats (en)	['nɛsta 'hɔ:lʲ‚plats]
terminus	slutstation (en)	['slʉt‚sta'ɧun]
schedule	tidtabell (en)	['tid ta'bɛlʲ]
to wait (vt)	att vänta	[at 'vɛnta]
ticket	biljett (en)	[bi'lʲet]
fare	biljettpris (ett)	[bi'lʲet‚pris]
cashier (ticket seller)	kassör (en)	[ka'sø:r]
ticket inspection	biljettkontroll (en)	[bi'lʲet kɔn'trolʲ]
ticket inspector	kontrollant (en)	[kɔntrɔ'lʲant]
to be late (for ...)	att komma för sent	[at 'kɔma før 'sɛnt]
to miss (~ the train, etc.)	att komma för sent till ...	[at 'kɔma før 'sɛnt tilʲ ...]
to be in a hurry	att skynda sig	[at 'ɧynda sɛj]
taxi, cab	taxi (en)	['taksi]
taxi driver	taxichaufför (en)	['taksi ɧɔ'fø:r]
by taxi	med taxi	[me 'taksi]
taxi stand	taxihållplats (en)	['taksi 'hɔ:lʲ‚plʲats]
to call a taxi	att ringa efter taxi	[at 'riŋa ‚ɛftə 'taksi]
to take a taxi	att ta en taxi	[at ta en 'taksi]
traffic	trafik (en)	[tra'fik]
traffic jam	trafikstopp (ett)	[tra'fik‚stɔp]
rush hour	rusningstid (en)	['rusniŋs‚tid]
to park (vi)	att parkera	[at par'kera]
to park (vt)	att parkera	[at par'kera]
parking lot	parkeringsplats (en)	[par'keriŋs‚plʲats]
subway	tunnelbana (en)	['tunəlʲ‚bana]
station	station (en)	[sta'ɧun]

to take the subway	att ta tunnelbanan	[at ta 'tunəlɪˌbanan]
train	tåg (ett)	['toːg]
train station	tågstation (en)	['toːgˌstaˈɧʊn]

28. City. Life in the city

city, town	stad (en)	['stad]
capital city	huvudstad (en)	['huːvʉdˌstad]
village	by (en)	['by]

city map	stadskarta (en)	['stadsˌkaːʈa]
downtown	centrum (ett)	['sɛntrum]
suburb	förort (en)	['førˌʊːt]
suburban (adj)	förorts-	['førˌʊːʈs-]

outskirts	utkant (en)	['ʉtˌkant]
environs (suburbs)	omgivningar (pl)	['ɔmˌjiːvniŋar]
city block	kvarter (ett)	[kvaˈʈər]
residential block (area)	bostadskvarter (ett)	['bʊstadsˌkvaˈʈər]

traffic	trafik (en)	[traˈfik]
traffic lights	trafikljus (ett)	[traˈfikjʉːs]
public transportation	offentlig transport (en)	[ɔˈfɛntli transˈpoːʈ]
intersection	korsning (en)	['kɔːʂniŋ]

crosswalk	övergångsställe (ett)	['øːvɛrgɔŋsˌstɛlʲe]
pedestrian underpass	gångtunnel (en)	['gɔŋˌtunəlʲ]
to cross (~ the street)	att gå över	[at 'goː 'øːvɛr]
pedestrian	fotgängare (en)	['fʊtˌjenarə]
sidewalk	trottoar (en)	[trɔtʊ'ar]

bridge	bro (en)	['brʊ]
embankment (river walk)	kaj (en)	['kaj]
fountain	fontän (en)	[fɔn'tɛn]

allée (garden walkway)	allé (en)	[a'lʲeː]
park	park (en)	['park]
boulevard	boulevard (en)	[bʊlʲe'vaːd]
square	torg (ett)	['tɔrj]
avenue (wide street)	aveny (en)	[ave'ny]
street	gata (en)	['gata]
side street	sidogata (en)	['sidʊˌgata]
dead end	återvändsgränd (en)	['oːtɛrvɛnsˌgrɛnd]

house	hus (ett)	['hʉs]
building	byggnad (en)	['bygnad]
skyscraper	skyskrapa (en)	['ɧyˌskrapa]

| facade | fasad (en) | [fa'sad] |
| roof | tak (ett) | ['tak] |

window	fönster (ett)	['fœnstər]
arch	båge (en)	['boːgə]
column	kolonn (en)	[kʊ'lʲɔn]
corner	knut (en)	['knʉt]

store window	skyltfönster (ett)	['ɦylʲt,fœnstər]
signboard (store sign, etc.)	skylt (en)	['ɦylʲt]
poster	affisch (en)	[a'fiːʃ]
advertising poster	reklamplakat (ett)	[rɛ'klʲam,plʲa'kat]
billboard	reklamskylt (en)	[rɛ'klʲam,ɦylʲt]

garbage, trash	sopor, avfall (ett)	['sʊpʊr], ['avfalʲ]
trashcan (public ~)	soptunna (en)	['sʊp,tuna]
to litter (vi)	att skräpa ner	[at 'skrɛːpa ner]
garbage dump	soptipp (en)	['sʊp,tip]

phone booth	telefonkiosk (en)	[telʲe'fɔn,ɕøsk]
lamppost	lyktstolpe (en)	['lʲyk,stolʲpə]
bench (park ~)	bänk (ett)	['bɛŋk]

police officer	polis (en)	[pʊ'lis]
police	polis (en)	[pʊ'lis]
beggar	tiggare (en)	['tigarə]
homeless (n)	hemlös (ett)	['hɛmlʲøːs]

29. Urban institutions

store	affär, butik (en)	[a'fæːr], [bu'tik]
drugstore, pharmacy	apotek (ett)	[apʊ'tek]
eyeglass store	optiker (en)	['ɔptikər]
shopping mall	köpcenter (ett)	['ɕøːp,sɛntɛr]
supermarket	snabbköp (ett)	['snab,ɕøːp]

bakery	bageri (ett)	[bage'riː]
baker	bagare (en)	['bagarə]
pastry shop	konditori (ett)	[kɔnditʊ'riː]
grocery store	speceriaffär (en)	[spese'ri a'fæːr]
butcher shop	slaktare butik (en)	['slʲaktarə bu'tik]

| produce store | grönsakshandel (en) | ['grøːnsaks,handəlʲ] |
| market | marknad (en) | ['marknad] |

coffee house	kafé (ett)	[ka'feː]
restaurant	restaurang (en)	[rɛstɔ'raŋ]
pub, bar	pub (en)	['pub]
pizzeria	pizzeria (en)	[pitse'ria]

hair salon	frisersalong (en)	['frisər ʂa,lʲɔŋ]
post office	post (en)	['pɔst]
dry cleaners	kemtvätt (en)	['ɕemtvæt]

photo studio	fotoateljé (en)	['fʊtʊ atə‚lje:]
shoe store	skoaffär (en)	['skʊ:a‚fæ:r]
bookstore	bokhandel (en)	['bʊk‚handəlʲ]
sporting goods store	sportaffär (en)	['spɔ:ʈ a'fæ:r]

clothes repair shop	klädreparationer (en)	['klʲɛd 'repara‚ɧʊnər]
formal wear rental	kläduthyrning (en)	['klʲɛd ʉ'ty:ɳiŋ]
video rental store	filmuthyrning (en)	['filʲm ʉ'ty:ɳiŋ]

circus	cirkus (en)	['sirkʉs]
zoo	zoo (ett)	['sʊ:]
movie theater	biograf (en)	[biʊ'graf]
museum	museum (ett)	[mʉ'seʊm]
library	bibliotek (ett)	[bibliʊ'tek]

theater	teater (en)	[te'atər]
opera (opera house)	opera (en)	['ʊpera]
nightclub	nattklubb (en)	['nat‚klʉb]
casino	kasino (ett)	[ka'sinʊ]

mosque	moské (en)	[mʊs'ke:]
synagogue	synagoga (en)	['syna‚gɔga]
cathedral	katedral (en)	[katɛ'dralʲ]
temple	tempel (ett)	['tɛmpəlʲ]
church	kyrka (en)	['ɕyrka]

college	institut (ett)	[insti'tʉt]
university	universitet (ett)	[univɛʂi'tet]
school	skola (en)	['skʊlʲa]

prefecture	prefektur (en)	[prefɛk'tʉ:r]
city hall	rådhus (en)	['rɔd‚hʉs]
hotel	hotell (ett)	[hʊ'tɛlʲ]
bank	bank (en)	['baŋk]

embassy	ambassad (en)	[amba'sad]
travel agency	resebyrå (en)	['reseby‚rɔ:]
information office	informationsbyrå (en)	[informa'ɧʊns by‚rɔ:]
currency exchange	växelkontor (ett)	['vɛksəlʲ kɔn'tʊr]

| subway | tunnelbana (en) | ['tunəlʲ‚bana] |
| hospital | sjukhus (ett) | ['ɧʉ:k‚hʉs] |

| gas station | bensinstation (en) | [bɛn'sin‚sta'ɧʊn] |
| parking lot | parkeringsplats (en) | [par'keriŋs‚plʲats] |

30. Signs

| signboard (store sign, etc.) | skylt (en) | ['ɧylʲt] |
| notice (door sign, etc.) | inskrift (en) | ['in‚skrift] |

poster	poster, löpsedel (en)	['pɔstər], ['løp,sedəlʲ]
direction sign	vägvisare (en)	['vɛːg,visarə]
arrow (sign)	pil (en)	['pilʲ]

caution	varning (en)	['vaːnɪŋ]
warning sign	varningsskylt (en)	['vaːnɪŋs ,ʃylʲt]
to warn (vt)	att varna	[at 'vaːɳa]

rest day (weekly ~)	fridag (en)	['friˌdag]
timetable (schedule)	tidtabell (en)	['tid ta'bɛlʲ]
opening hours	öppettider (pl)	['øpetˌtiːdər]

WELCOME!	VÄLKOMMEN!	['vɛlʲˌkɔmən]
ENTRANCE	INGÅNG	['inˌgɔŋ]
EXIT	UTGÅNG	['ʉtˌgɔŋ]

PUSH	TRYCK	['trʏk]
PULL	DRAG	['drag]
OPEN	ÖPPET	['øpet]
CLOSED	STÄNGT	['stɛŋt]

| WOMEN | DAMER | ['damər] |
| MEN | HERRAR | ['hɛ'rar] |

| DISCOUNTS | RABATT | [ra'bat] |
| SALE | REA | ['rea] |

| NEW! | NYHET! | ['nyhet] |
| FREE | GRATIS | ['gratis] |

ATTENTION!	OBS!	['ɔbs]
NO VACANCIES	FUllBOKAT	['fulʲˌbukat]
RESERVED	RESERVERAT	[resɛr'verat]

| ADMINISTRATION | ADMINISTRATION | [administra'ʃun] |
| STAFF ONLY | ENDAST PERSONAL | ['ɛndast pɛʂu'nalʲ] |

BEWARE OF THE DOG!	VARNING FÖR HUNDEN	['vaːnɪŋ før 'hundən]
NO SMOKING	RÖKNING FÖRBJUDEN	['rœknɪŋ før'bjʉːdən]
DO NOT TOUCH!	FÅR EJ VIDRÖRAS!	['foːr ej 'vidrøːras]

DANGEROUS	FARLIG	['faːl̩ig]
DANGER	FARA	['fara]
HIGH VOLTAGE	HÖGSPÄNNING	['høːgˌspɛnɪŋ]

| NO SWIMMING! | BADNING FÖRBJUDEN | ['badnɪŋ før'bjʉːdən] |
| OUT OF ORDER | UR FUNKTION | ['ʉr funk'ʃun] |

FLAMMABLE	BRANDFARLIG	['brandˌfaːl̩ig]
FORBIDDEN	FÖRBJUD	[før'bjʉːd]
NO TRESPASSING!	TIllTRÄDE FÖRBJUDET	['tilʲtrɛːdə før'bjʉːdət]
WET PAINT	NYMÅLAT	['nyˌmoːlʲat]

31. Shopping

to buy (purchase)	att köpa	[at 'ɕøːpa]
purchase	inköp (ett)	['inˌɕøːp]
to go shopping	att shoppa	[at 'ʃɔpa]
shopping	shopping (en)	['ʃɔpiŋ]
to be open (ab. store)	att vara öppen	[at 'vara 'øpən]
to be closed	att vara stängd	[at 'vara stɛŋd]
footwear, shoes	skodon (pl)	['skʊdʊn]
clothes, clothing	kläder (pl)	['klʲɛːdər]
cosmetics	kosmetika (en)	[kɔs'mɛtika]
food products	matvaror (pl)	['matˌvarʊr]
gift, present	gåva, present (en)	['goːva], [pre'sɛnt]
salesman	försäljare (en)	[fœ:'ʂɛljarə]
saleswoman	försäljare (en)	[fœ:'ʂɛljarə]
check out, cash desk	kassa (en)	['kasa]
mirror	spegel (en)	['spegəlʲ]
counter (store ~)	disk (en)	['disk]
fitting room	provrum (ett)	['prʊvˌruːm]
to try on	att prova	[at 'prʊva]
to fit (ab. dress, etc.)	att passa	[at 'pasa]
to like (I like ...)	att gilla	[at 'jilʲa]
price	pris (ett)	['pris]
price tag	prislapp (en)	['prisˌlʲap]
to cost (vt)	att kosta	[at 'kɔsta]
How much?	Hur mycket?	[hʉr 'mʏkə]
discount	rabatt (en)	[ra'bat]
inexpensive (adj)	billig	['bilig]
cheap (adj)	billig	['bilig]
expensive (adj)	dyr	['dyr]
It's expensive	Det är dyrt	[dɛ æːr 'dyːt]
rental (n)	uthyrning (en)	['ʉtˌhyŋiŋ]
to rent (~ a tuxedo)	att hyra	[at 'hyra]
credit (trade credit)	kredit (en)	[kre'dit]
on credit (adv)	på kredit	[pɔ kre'dit]

CLOTHING & ACCESSORIES

32. Outerwear. Coats

clothes	kläder (pl)	['klʲɛ:dər]
outerwear	ytterkläder	['ytə͵klʲɛ:dər]
winter clothing	vinterkläder (pl)	['vintə͵klʲɛ:dər]
coat (overcoat)	rock, kappa (en)	['rɔk], ['kapa]
fur coat	päls (en)	['pɛlʲs]
fur jacket	pälsjacka (en)	['pɛlʲs͵jaka]
down coat	dunjacka (en)	['dɵ:n͵jaka]
jacket (e.g., leather ~)	jacka (en)	['jaka]
raincoat (trenchcoat, etc.)	regnrock (en)	['rɛgn͵rɔk]
waterproof (adj)	vattentät	['vatən͵tɛt]

33. Men's & women's clothing

shirt (button shirt)	skjorta (en)	['ʂu:ʈa]
pants	byxor (pl)	['byksʊr]
jeans	jeans (en)	['jins]
suit jacket	kavaj (en)	[ka'vaj]
suit	kostym (en)	[kɔs'tym]
dress (frock)	klänning (en)	['klʲɛniŋ]
skirt	kjol (en)	['çø:lʲ]
blouse	blus (en)	['blɵ:s]
knitted jacket (cardigan, etc.)	stickad tröja (en)	['stikad 'trøja]
jacket (of woman's suit)	dräktjacka, kavaj (en)	['drɛkt 'jaka], ['kavaj]
T-shirt	T-shirt (en)	['ti:͵ʃɔ:ʈ]
shorts (short trousers)	shorts (en)	['ʃɔ:ts]
tracksuit	träningsoverall (en)	['trɛ:niŋs ove'rɔ:lʲ]
bathrobe	morgonrock (en)	['mɔrgɔn͵rɔk]
pajamas	pyjamas (en)	[py'jamas]
sweater	sweater, tröja (en)	['svitər], ['trøja]
pullover	pullover (en)	[pu'lʲɔ:vər]
vest	väst (en)	['vɛst]
tailcoat	frack (en)	['frak]
tuxedo	smoking (en)	['smɔkiŋ]

uniform	uniform (en)	[uni'fɔrm]
workwear	arbetskläder (pl)	['arbets,kl'ɛ:dər]
overalls	overall (en)	['ɔve,rɔ:l']
coat (e.g., doctor's smock)	rock (en)	['rɔk]

34. Clothing. Underwear

underwear	underkläder (pl)	['undə,kl'ɛ:dər]
boxers, briefs	underbyxor (pl)	['undə,byksʊr]
panties	trosor (pl)	['trʊsʊr]
undershirt (A-shirt)	undertröja (en)	['undə,trøja]
socks	sockor (pl)	['sɔkʊr]

nightgown	nattlinne (ett)	['nat,linə]
bra	behå (en)	[be'hɔ:]
knee highs (knee-high socks)	knästrumpor (pl)	['knɛ:,strumpʊr]
pantyhose	strumpbyxor (pl)	['strump,byksʊr]
stockings (thigh highs)	strumpor (pl)	['strumpʊr]
bathing suit	baddräkt (en)	['bad,drɛkt]

35. Headwear

hat	hatt (en)	['hat]
fedora	hatt (en)	['hat]
baseball cap	baseballkeps (en)	['bejsbɔl' keps]
flatcap	keps (en)	['keps]

beret	basker (en)	['baskər]
hood	luva, kapuschong (en)	['lʉ:va], [kapʉ'ʃɔ:ŋ]
panama hat	panamahatt (en)	['panama,hat]
knit cap (knitted hat)	luva (en)	['lʉ:va]

headscarf	sjalett (en)	[ʃa'l'et]
women's hat	hatt (en)	['hat]
hard hat	hjälm (en)	['jɛl'm]
garrison cap	båtmössa (en)	['bɔt,mœsa]
helmet	hjälm (en)	['jɛl'm]

| derby | plommonstop (ett) | ['pl'ʉmɔn,stʊp] |
| top hat | hög hatt, cylinder (en) | ['hø:g ,hat], [sy'lindər] |

36. Footwear

| footwear | skodon (pl) | ['skʊdʊn] |
| shoes (men's shoes) | skor (pl) | ['skʊr] |

shoes (women's shoes)	damskor (pl)	['dam,skʊr]
boots (e.g., cowboy ~)	stövlar (pl)	['støvlʲar]
slippers	tofflor (pl)	['tɔflʲʊr]

tennis shoes (e.g., Nike ~)	tennisskor (pl)	['tɛnis,skʊr]
sneakers (e.g., Converse ~)	canvas skor (pl)	['kanvas ,skʊr]
sandals	sandaler (pl)	[san'dalʲer]

cobbler (shoe repairer)	skomakare (en)	['skʊ,makarə]
heel	klack (en)	['klʲak]
pair (of shoes)	par (ett)	['par]

shoestring	skosnöre (ett)	['skʊ,snø:rə]
to lace (vt)	att snöra	[at 'snø:ra]
shoehorn	skohorn (ett)	['skʊ,hʊ:n]
shoe polish	skokräm (en)	['skʊ,krɛm]

37. Personal accessories

gloves	handskar (pl)	['hanskar]
mittens	vantar (pl)	['vantar]
scarf (muffler)	halsduk (en)	['halʲs,dɵ:k]

glasses (eyeglasses)	glasögon (pl)	['glʲas,ø:gɔn]
frame (eyeglass ~)	båge (en)	['bo:gə]
umbrella	paraply (ett)	[para'plʲy]
walking stick	käpp (en)	['ɕɛp]

| hairbrush | hårborste (en) | ['ho:r,bo:ʂtə] |
| fan | solfjäder (en) | ['sʊlʲ,fjɛ:dər] |

| tie (necktie) | slips (en) | ['slips] |
| bow tie | fluga (en) | ['flɵ:ga] |

| suspenders | hängslen (pl) | ['hɛŋslʲən] |
| handkerchief | näsduk (en) | ['nɛs,dɵk] |

| comb | kam (en) | ['kam] |
| barrette | hårklämma (ett) | ['ho:r,klʲɛma] |

| hairpin | hårnål (en) | ['ho:,ɳo:lʲ] |
| buckle | spänne (ett) | ['spɛnə] |

| belt | bälte (ett) | ['bɛlʲtə] |
| shoulder strap | rem (en) | ['rem] |

bag (handbag)	väska (en)	['vɛska]
purse	damväska (en)	['dam,vɛska]
backpack	ryggsäck (en)	['rʏg,sɛk]

38. Clothing. Miscellaneous

fashion	mode (ett)	['mʊdə]
in vogue (adj)	modern	[mʊ'dɛ:n]
fashion designer	modedesigner (en)	['mʊdə de'sajnər]
collar	krage (en)	['kragə]
pocket	ficka (en)	['fika]
pocket (as adj)	fick-	['fik-]
sleeve	ärm (en)	['æ:rm]
hanging loop	hängband (ett)	['hɛŋ band]
fly (on trousers)	gylf (en)	['gylʲf]
zipper (fastener)	blixtlås (ett)	['blikst,lʲo:s]
fastener	knäppning (en)	['knɛpniŋ]
button	knapp (en)	['knap]
buttonhole	knapphål (ett)	['knap,ho:lʲ]
to come off (ab. button)	att lossna	[at 'lʲɔsna]
to sew (vi, vt)	att sy	[at sy]
to embroider (vi, vt)	att brodera	[at brʊ'dera]
embroidery	broderi (ett)	[brʊde'ri:]
sewing needle	synål (en)	['sy,no:lʲ]
thread	tråd (en)	['tro:d]
seam	söm (en)	['sø:m]
to get dirty (vi)	att smutsa ned sig	[at 'smutsa ned sɛj]
stain (mark, spot)	fläck (en)	['flʲɛk]
to crease, crumple (vi)	att bli skrynklig	[at bli 'skrʏŋklig]
to tear, to rip (vt)	att riva	[at 'riva]
clothes moth	mal (en)	['malʲ]

39. Personal care. Cosmetics

toothpaste	tandkräm (en)	['tand,krɛm]
toothbrush	tandborste (en)	['tand,bɔ:ʂtə]
to brush one's teeth	att borsta tänderna	[at 'bɔ:ʂta 'tɛndɛ:ɳa]
razor	hyvel (en)	['hyvəlʲ]
shaving cream	rakkräm (en)	['rak,krɛm]
to shave (vi)	att raka sig	[at 'raka sɛj]
soap	tvål (en)	['tvo:lʲ]
shampoo	schampo (ett)	['ɧam,pʊ]
scissors	sax (en)	['saks]
nail file	nagelfil (en)	['nagəlʲ,filʲ]
nail clippers	nageltång (en)	['nagəlʲ,tɔŋ]
tweezers	pincett (en)	[pin'sɛt]

cosmetics	kosmetika (en)	[kɔs'mɛtika]
face mask	ansiktsmask (en)	[an'sikts‚mask]
manicure	manikyr (en)	[mani'kyr]
to have a manicure	att få manikyr	[at fo: mani'kyr]
pedicure	pedikyr (en)	[pedi'kyr]

make-up bag	kosmetikväska (en)	[kɔsmɛ'tik‚vɛska]
face powder	puder (ett)	['pʉ:dər]
powder compact	puderdosa (en)	['pʉ:dɛ‚dɔ:sa]
blusher	rouge (ett)	['ru:ʃ]

perfume (bottled)	parfym (en)	[par'fym]
toilet water (lotion)	eau de toilette (en)	['ɔ:detua‚lʲet]
lotion	rakvatten (ett)	['rak‚vatən]
cologne	eau de cologne (en)	['ɔ:dekɔ‚lʲɔnʲ]

eyeshadow	ögonskugga (en)	['ø:gɔn‚skuga]
eyeliner	ögonpenna (en)	['ø:gɔn‚pɛna]
mascara	mascara (en)	[ma'skara]

lipstick	läppstift (ett)	['lʲɛp‚stift]
nail polish, enamel	nagellack (ett)	['nagəlʲ‚lʲak]
hair spray	hårspray (en)	['ho:r‚sprɛj]
deodorant	deodorant (en)	[deʊdʊ'rant]

cream	kräm (en)	['krɛm]
face cream	ansiktskräm (en)	[an'sikts‚krɛm]
hand cream	handkräm (en)	['hand‚krɛm]
anti-wrinkle cream	anti-rynkor kräm (en)	['anti‚rʏnkʊr 'krɛm]
day cream	dagkräm (en)	['dag‚krɛm]
night cream	nattkräm (en)	['nat‚krɛm]
day (as adj)	dag-	['dag-]
night (as adj)	natt-	['nat-]

tampon	tampong (en)	[tam'pɔŋ]
toilet paper (toilet roll)	toalettpapper (ett)	[tʊa'lʲet‚papər]
hair dryer	hårtork (en)	['ho:‚tʊrk]

40. Watches. Clocks

watch (wristwatch)	armbandsur (ett)	['armbands‚ʉ:r]
dial	urtavla (en)	['ʉ:‚tavlʲa]
hand (of clock, watch)	visare (en)	['visarə]
metal watch band	armband (ett)	['arm‚band]
watch strap	armband (ett)	['arm‚band]

battery	batteri (ett)	[batɛ'ri:]
to be dead (battery)	att bli urladdad	[at bli 'ʉ:‚lʲadad]
to change a battery	att byta batteri	[at 'byta batɛ'ri:]
to run fast	att gå för fort	[at 'go: før 'fo:t]

to run slow	att gå för långsamt	[at 'go: før 'lɔŋˌsamt]
wall clock	väggklocka (en)	['vɛɡˌklʲɔka]
hourglass	sandklocka (en)	['sandˌklʲɔka]
sundial	solklocka (en)	['sʊlʲˌklʲɔka]
alarm clock	väckarklocka (en)	['vɛkarˌklʲɔka]
watchmaker	urmakare (en)	['ʉrˌmakarə]
to repair (vt)	att reparera	[at repa'rera]

EVERYDAY EXPERIENCE

41. Money

money	pengar (pl)	['pɛŋar]
currency exchange	växling (en)	['vɛksliŋ]
exchange rate	kurs (en)	['kuːʂ]
ATM	bankomat (en)	[baŋkʊ'mat]
coin	mynt (ett)	['mʏnt]

| dollar | dollar (en) | ['dɔlʲar] |
| euro | euro (en) | ['ɛvrɔ] |

lira	lire (en)	['lirə]
Deutschmark	mark (en)	['mark]
franc	franc (en)	['fran]
pound sterling	pund sterling (ett)	['puŋ stɛr'liŋ]
yen	yen (en)	['jɛn]

debt	skuld (en)	['skʉlʲd]
debtor	gäldenär (en)	[jɛlʲdɛ'næːr]
to lend (money)	att låna ut	[at 'lʲoːna ʉt]
to borrow (vi, vt)	att låna	[at 'lʲoːna]

bank	bank (en)	['baŋk]
account	konto (ett)	['kɔntʊ]
to deposit (vt)	att sätta in	[at 'sæta in]
to deposit into the account	att sätta in på kontot	[at 'sæta in pɔ 'kɔntʊt]
to withdraw (vt)	att ta ut från kontot	[at ta ʉt frɔn 'kɔntʊt]

credit card	kreditkort (ett)	[kre'dit̩koːt]
cash	kontanter (pl)	[kɔn'tantər]
check	check (en)	['ɕɛk]
to write a check	att skriva en check	[at 'skriva en 'ɕɛk]
checkbook	checkbok (en)	['ɕɛk̩bʊk]

wallet	plånbok (en)	['plʲoːn̩bʊk]
change purse	börs (en)	['bøːʂ]
safe	säkerhetsskåp (ett)	['sɛːkərhets̩skoːp]

heir	arvinge (en)	['arviŋə]
inheritance	arv (ett)	['arv]
fortune (wealth)	förmögenhet (en)	[før'møgən̩het]

| lease | hyra (en) | ['hyra] |
| rent (money) | hyra (en) | ['hyra] |

to rent (sth from sb)	att hyra	[at 'hyra]
price	pris (ett)	['pris]
cost	kostnad (en)	['kɔstnad]
sum	summa (en)	['suma]
to spend (vt)	att lägga ut	[at 'lɛga ʉt]
expenses	utgifter (pl)	['ʉtˌjiftər]
to economize (vi, vt)	att spara	[at 'spara]
economical	sparsam	['spaːʂam]
to pay (vi, vt)	att betala	[at be'talʲa]
payment	betalning (en)	[be'talʲniŋ]
change (give the ~)	växel (en)	['vɛksəlʲ]
tax	skatt (en)	['skat]
fine	bot (en)	['bʊt]
to fine (vt)	att bötfälla	[at 'bøtˌfɛlʲa]

42. Post. Postal service

post office	post (en)	['pɔst]
mail (letters, etc.)	post (en)	['pɔst]
mailman	brevbärare (en)	['brevˌbæːrarə]
opening hours	öppettider (pl)	['øpetˌtiːdər]
letter	brev (ett)	['brev]
registered letter	rekommenderat brev (ett)	[rekɔmən'derat brev]
postcard	postkort (ett)	['pɔstˌkɔːt]
telegram	telegram (ett)	[telʲe'gram]
package (parcel)	postpaket (ett)	['pɔst paˌket]
money transfer	pengaöverföring (en)	['pɛŋaˌøvə'føːriŋ]
to receive (vt)	att ta emot	[at ta ɛmoːt]
to send (vt)	att skicka	[at 'ɧika]
sending	avsändning (en)	['avˌsɛndniŋ]
address	adress (en)	[a'drɛs]
ZIP code	postnummer (ett)	['pɔstˌnumər]
sender	avsändare (en)	['avˌsɛndarə]
receiver	mottagare (en)	['mɔtˌtagarə]
name (first name)	förnamn (ett)	['fœːˌɳamn]
surname (last name)	efternamn (ett)	['ɛftəˌɳamn]
postage rate	tariff (en)	[ta'rif]
standard (adj)	vanlig	['vanlig]
economical (adj)	ekonomisk	[ɛkʊ'nɔmisk]
weight	vikt (en)	['vikt]
to weigh (~ letters)	att väga	[at 'vɛːga]

envelope	kuvert (ett)	[kʉːˈvær]
postage stamp	frimärke (ett)	[ˈfriˌmærkə]
to stamp an envelope	att sätta på frimärke	[at ˈsæta pɔ ˈfriˌmærkə]

43. Banking

| bank | bank (en) | [ˈbaŋk] |
| branch (of bank, etc.) | avdelning (en) | [avˈdɛlʲniŋ] |

| bank clerk, consultant | konsulent (en) | [kɔnsuˈlʲɛnt] |
| manager (director) | föreståndare (en) | [førəˈstɔndarə] |

bank account	bankkonto (ett)	[ˈbaŋkˌkɔntʉ]
account number	kontonummer (ett)	[ˈkɔntʉˌnumər]
checking account	checkkonto (ett)	[ˈɕɛkˌkɔntʉ]
savings account	sparkonto (ett)	[ˈsparˌkɔntʉ]

| to open an account | att öppna ett konto | [at ˈøpna ɛt ˈkɔntʉ] |
| to close the account | att avsluta kontot | [at ˈavˌslʉːta ˈkɔntʉt] |

| to deposit into the account | att sätta in på kontot | [at ˈsæta in pɔ ˈkɔntʉt] |
| to withdraw (vt) | att ta ut från kontot | [at ta ʉt frɔn ˈkɔntʉt] |

| deposit | insats (en) | [ˈinˌsats] |
| to make a deposit | att sätta in | [at ˈsæta in] |

| wire transfer | överföring (en) | [ˈøːvəˌføːriŋ] |
| to wire, to transfer | att överföra | [at øːvəˌføra] |

| sum | summa (en) | [ˈsuma] |
| How much? | Hur mycket? | [hʉr ˈmʏkə] |

| signature | signatur, underskrift (en) | [signaˈtʉːr], [ˈundəˌskrift] |
| to sign (vt) | att underteckna | [at ˈundəˌtɛkna] |

| credit card | kreditkort (ett) | [kreˈditˌkɔːʈ] |
| code (PIN code) | kod (en) | [ˈkɔd] |

| credit card number | kreditkortsnummer (ett) | [kreˈditˌkɔːʈs ˈnumər] |
| ATM | bankomat (en) | [baŋkʉˈmat] |

check	check (en)	[ˈɕɛk]
to write a check	att skriva en check	[at ˈskriva en ˈɕɛk]
checkbook	checkbok (en)	[ˈɕɛkˌbʉk]

loan (bank ~)	lån (ett)	[ˈlʲoːn]
to apply for a loan	att ansöka om lån	[at ˈanˌsøːka ɔm ˈlʲoːn]
to get a loan	att få ett lån	[at fo: et ˈlʲoːn]
to give a loan	att ge ett lån	[at je: et ˈlʲoːn]
guarantee	garanti (en)	[garanˈtiː]

44. Telephone. Phone conversation

telephone	telefon (en)	[telʲeˈfɔn]
cell phone	mobiltelefon (en)	[mɔˈbilʲ telʲeˈfɔn]
answering machine	telefonsvarare (en)	[telʲeˈfɔnˌsvararə]

| to call (by phone) | att ringa | [at ˈriŋa] |
| phone call | telefonsamtal (en) | [telʲeˈfɔnˌsamtalʲ] |

to dial a number	att slå nummer	[at ˈslʲoː ˈnumər]
Hello!	Hallå!	[haˈlʲoː]
to ask (vt)	att fråga	[at ˈfroːga]
to answer (vi, vt)	att svara	[at ˈsvara]

to hear (vt)	att höra	[at ˈhøːra]
well (adv)	gott, bra	[ˈgɔt], [ˈbra]
not well (adv)	dåligt	[ˈdoːlit]
noises (interference)	bruser, störningar (pl)	[ˈbrɵːsər], [ˈstøːɲiɳar]

receiver	telefonlur (en)	[telʲeˈfɔnˌlɵːr]
to pick up (~ the phone)	att lyfta telefonluren	[at ˈlʲyfta telʲeˈfɔn ˈlɵːrən]
to hang up (~ the phone)	att lägga på	[at ˈlʲɛga pɔ]

busy (engaged)	upptagen	[ˈupˌtagən]
to ring (ab. phone)	att ringa	[at ˈriŋa]
telephone book	telefonkatalog (en)	[telʲeˈfɔn kataˈlʲog]

local (adj)	lokal-	[lʲoˈkalʲ-]
local call	lokalsamtal (ett)	[lʲoˈkalʲˌsamtalʲ]
long distance (~ call)	riks-	[ˈriks-]
long-distance call	rikssamtal (ett)	[ˈriksˌsamtalʲ]
international (adj)	internationell	[ˈintɛːɳatʃʉˌnɛlʲ]
international call	internationell samtal (ett)	[ˈintɛːɳatʃʉˌnɛlʲ ˈsamtalʲ]

45. Cell phone

cell phone	mobiltelefon (en)	[mɔˈbilʲ telʲeˈfɔn]
display	skärm (en)	[ˈʃæːrm]
button	knapp (en)	[ˈknap]
SIM card	SIM-kort (ett)	[ˈsimˌkɔːt]

battery	batteri (ett)	[batɛˈriː]
to be dead (battery)	att bli urladdad	[at bli ˈɵːˌlʲadad]
charger	laddare (en)	[ˈlʲadarə]

menu	meny (en)	[meˈny]
settings	inställningar (pl)	[ˈinˌstɛlʲˈɲiɳar]
tune (melody)	melodi (en)	[melʲoˈdiː]
to select (vt)	att välja	[at ˈvɛlja]

calculator	kalkylator (en)	[kalˈkyˈlʲatʊr]
voice mail	telefonsvarare (en)	[telʲeˈfɔnˌsvararə]
alarm clock	väckarklocka, alarm (en)	[ˈvɛkarˌklʲɔka], [aˈlʲarm]
contacts	kontakter (pl)	[kɔnˈtaktər]

| SMS (text message) | SMS meddelande (ett) | [ɛsɛˈmɛs meˈdelʲandə] |
| subscriber | abonnent (en) | [abɔˈnɛnt] |

46. Stationery

| ballpoint pen | kulspetspenna (en) | [ˈkʉlʲspetsˌpɛna] |
| fountain pen | reservoarpenna (en) | [resɛrvʊˈarˌpɛna] |

pencil	blyertspenna (en)	[ˈblʲyɛːˌʦˌpɛna]
highlighter	märkpenna (en)	[ˈmœrkˌpɛna]
felt-tip pen	tuschpenna (en)	[ˈtuːʃˌpɛna]

| notepad | block (ett) | [ˈblʲɔk] |
| agenda (diary) | dagbok (en) | [ˈdagˌbʉk] |

ruler	linjal (en)	[liˈnjalʲ]
calculator	kalkylator (en)	[kalˈkyˈlʲatʊr]
eraser	suddgummi (ett)	[ˈsudˌgumi]
thumbtack	häftstift (ett)	[ˈhɛftˌstift]
paper clip	gem (ett)	[ˈgem]

glue	lim (ett)	[ˈlim]
stapler	häftapparat (en)	[ˈhɛft apaˌrat]
hole punch	hålslag (ett)	[ˈhoːlʲˌslʲag]
pencil sharpener	pennvässare (en)	[ˈpɛnˌvɛsarə]

47. Foreign languages

language	språk (ett)	[ˈsproːk]
foreign (adj)	främmande	[ˈfrɛmandə]
foreign language	främmande språk (ett)	[ˈfrɛmandə sproːk]
to study (vt)	att studera	[at stuˈdera]
to learn (language, etc.)	att lära sig	[at ˈlʲæːra sɛj]

to read (vi, vt)	att läsa	[at ˈlʲɛːsa]
to speak (vi, vt)	att tala	[at ˈtalʲa]
to understand (vt)	att förstå	[at fœːˈstoː]
to write (vt)	att skriva	[at ˈskriva]

fast (adv)	snabbt	[ˈsnabt]
slowly (adv)	långsamt	[ˈlʲɔŋˌsamt]
fluently (adv)	flytande	[ˈflʲytandə]
rules	regler (pl)	[ˈrɛglʲər]

grammar	grammatik (en)	[grama'tik]
vocabulary	ordförråd (ett)	['ʊːdfœːˌroːd]
phonetics	fonetik (en)	[fone'tik]

textbook	lärobok (en)	['lʲæːrʊˌbʊk]
dictionary	ordbok (en)	['ʊːdˌbʊk]
teach-yourself book	självinstruerande lärobok (en)	['ɧɛlʲv instrʉ'ɛrandə 'lʲæːrʊˌbʊk]
phrasebook	parlör (en)	[paː'lʲøːr]

cassette, tape	kassett (en)	[ka'sɛt]
videotape	videokassett (en)	['videʊ ka'sɛt]
CD, compact disc	cd-skiva (en)	['sede ˌɧiva]
DVD	dvd (en)	[deve'deː]

alphabet	alfabet (ett)	['alʲfabet]
to spell (vt)	att stava	[at 'stava]
pronunciation	uttal (ett)	['ʉtˌtalʲ]

accent	brytning (en)	['brʏtniŋ]
with an accent	med brytning	[me 'brʏtniŋ]
without an accent	utan brytning	['ʉtan 'brʏtniŋ]

| word | ord (ett) | ['ʊːd] |
| meaning | betydelse (en) | [be'tydəlʲsə] |

course (e.g., a French ~)	kurs (en)	['kuːʂ]
to sign up	att anmäla sig	[at 'anˌmɛːlʲa sɛj]
teacher	lärare (en)	['lʲæːrarə]

translation (process)	översättning (en)	['øːvəˌsætniŋ]
translation (text, etc.)	översättning (en)	['øːvəˌsætniŋ]
translator	översättare (en)	['øːvəˌsætarə]
interpreter	tolk (en)	['tolʲk]

| polyglot | polyglott (en) | [pulʏ'glʲot] |
| memory | minne (ett) | ['minə] |

MEALS. RESTAURANT

48. Table setting

spoon	sked (en)	['ɧed]
knife	kniv (en)	['kniv]
fork	gaffel (en)	['gafəlʲ]
cup (e.g., coffee ~)	kopp (en)	['kop]
plate (dinner ~)	tallrik (en)	['talʲrik]
saucer	tefat (ett)	['te,fat]
napkin (on table)	servett (en)	[sɛr'vɛt]
toothpick	tandpetare (en)	['tand,petarə]

49. Restaurant

restaurant	restaurang (en)	[rɛsto'raŋ]
coffee house	kafé (ett)	[ka'fe:]
pub, bar	bar (en)	['bar]
tearoom	tehus (ett)	['te:,hʉs]
waiter	servitör (en)	[sɛrvi'tø:r]
waitress	servitris (en)	[sɛrvi'tris]
bartender	bartender (en)	['ba:,ʈɛndər]
menu	meny (en)	[me'ny]
wine list	vinlista (en)	['vin,lista]
to book a table	att reservera bord	[at resɛr'vera bʉ:d]
course, dish	rätt (en)	['ræt]
to order (meal)	att beställa	[at be'stɛlʲa]
to make an order	att beställa	[at be'stɛlʲa]
aperitif	aperitif (en)	[aperi'tif]
appetizer	förrätt (en)	['fœ:ræt]
dessert	dessert (en)	[dɛ'sɛ:r]
check	nota (en)	['nʊta]
to pay the check	att betala notan	[at be'talʲa 'nʊtan]
to give change	att ge tillbaka växel	[at je: tilʲ'baka 'vɛksəlʲ]
tip	dricks (en)	['driks]

50. Meals

food	**mat (en)**	['mat]
to eat (vi, vt)	**att äta**	[at 'ɛ:ta]
breakfast	**frukost (en)**	['frʉ:kɔst]
to have breakfast	**att äta frukost**	[at 'ɛ:ta 'frʉ:kɔst]
lunch	**lunch (en)**	['lʉnɕ]
to have lunch	**att äta lunch**	[at 'ɛ:ta ˌlʉnɕ]
dinner	**kvällsmat (en)**	['kvɛlˈsˌmat]
to have dinner	**att äta kvällsmat**	[at 'ɛ:ta 'kvɛlˈsˌmat]
appetite	**aptit (en)**	['aptit]
Enjoy your meal!	**Smaklig måltid!**	['smaklig 'mo:lˈtid]
to open (~ a bottle)	**att öppna**	[at 'øpna]
to spill (liquid)	**att spilla**	[at 'spilˈa]
to spill out (vi)	**att spillas ut**	[at 'spilˈas ʉt]
to boil (vi)	**att koka**	[at 'kʊka]
to boil (vt)	**att koka**	[at 'kʊka]
boiled (~ water)	**kokt**	['kʊkt]
to chill, cool down (vt)	**att avkyla**	[at 'avˌɕylˈa]
to chill (vi)	**att avkylas**	[at 'avˌɕylˈas]
taste, flavor	**smak (en)**	['smak]
aftertaste	**bismak (en)**	['bismak]
to slim down (lose weight)	**att vara på diet**	[at 'vara pɔ di'et]
diet	**diet (en)**	[di'et]
vitamin	**vitamin (ett)**	[vita'min]
calorie	**kalori (en)**	[kalˈɔ'ri:]
vegetarian (n)	**vegetarian (en)**	[vegetiri'an]
vegetarian (adj)	**vegetarisk**	[vege'tarisk]
fats (nutrient)	**fett (ett)**	['fɛt]
proteins	**proteiner (pl)**	[prɔte'i:nər]
carbohydrates	**kolhydrater (pl)**	['kɔlˈhyˌdratər]
slice (of lemon, ham)	**skiva (en)**	['ɧiva]
piece (of cake, pie)	**bit (en)**	['bit]
crumb	**smula (en)**	['smʉlˈa]
(of bread, cake, etc.)		

51. Cooked dishes

course, dish	**rätt (en)**	['ræt]
cuisine	**kök (ett)**	['ɕø:k]
recipe	**recept (ett)**	[re'sɛpt]
portion	**portion (en)**	[pɔ:[ˈɧʊn]

| salad | sallad (en) | ['salʲad] |
| soup | soppa (en) | ['sɔpa] |

clear soup (broth)	buljong (en)	[bu'ljɔŋ]
sandwich (bread)	smörgås (en)	['smœr͵gɔːs]
fried eggs	stekt ägg (en)	['stɛkt ͵ɛg]

| hamburger (beefburger) | hamburgare (en) | ['hamburgarə] |
| beefsteak | biffstek (en) | ['bif͵stɛk] |

side dish	tillbehör (ett)	['tilʲbe͵hør]
spaghetti	spagetti	[spa'gɛti]
mashed potatoes	potatismos (ett)	[pʊ'tatis͵mʊs]
pizza	pizza (en)	['pitsa]
porridge (oatmeal, etc.)	gröt (en)	['grøːt]
omelet	omelett (en)	[ɔmə'lʲet]

boiled (e.g., ~ beef)	kokt	['kʊkt]
smoked (adj)	rökt	['rœkt]
fried (adj)	stekt	['stɛkt]
dried (adj)	torkad	['tɔrkad]
frozen (adj)	fryst	['frʏst]
pickled (adj)	sylt-	['sylʲt-]

sweet (sugary)	söt	['søːt]
salty (adj)	salt	['salʲt]
cold (adj)	kall	['kalʲ]
hot (adj)	het, varm	['het], ['varm]
bitter (adj)	bitter	['bitər]
tasty (adj)	läcker	['lʲɛkər]

to cook in boiling water	att koka	[at 'kʊka]
to cook (dinner)	att laga	[at 'lʲaga]
to fry (vt)	att steka	[at 'steka]
to heat up (food)	att värma upp	[at 'væːrma up]

to salt (vt)	att salta	[at 'salʲta]
to pepper (vt)	att peppra	[at 'pepra]
to grate (vt)	att riva	[at 'riva]
peel (n)	skal (ett)	['skalʲ]
to peel (vt)	att skala	[at 'skalʲa]

52. Food

meat	kött (ett)	['ɕœt]
chicken	höna (en)	['høːna]
Rock Cornish hen (poussin)	kyckling (en)	['ɕykliŋ]
duck	anka (en)	['aŋka]
goose	gås (en)	['goːs]

game	vilt (ett)	['vilʲt]
turkey	kalkon (en)	[kalʲ'kʊn]

pork	fläsk (ett)	['flʲɛsk]
veal	kalvkött (en)	['kalʲv‚ɕœt]
lamb	lammkött (ett)	['lʲam‚ɕœt]
beef	oxkött, nötkött (ett)	['ʊks‚ɕœt], ['nøːt‚ɕœt]
rabbit	kanin (en)	[ka'nin]

sausage (bologna, pepperoni, etc.)	korv (en)	['kɔrv]
vienna sausage (frankfurter)	wienerkorv (en)	['viŋɛr‚kɔrv]
bacon	bacon (ett)	['bɛjkɔn]
ham	skinka (en)	['ɧiŋka]
gammon	skinka (en)	['ɧiŋka]

pâté	paté (en)	[pa'te]
liver	lever (en)	['lʲevər]
hamburger (ground beef)	köttfärs (en)	['ɕœt‚fæːʂ]
tongue	tunga (en)	['tuŋa]

egg	ägg (ett)	['ɛg]
eggs	ägg (pl)	['ɛg]
egg white	äggvita (en)	['ɛg‚viːta]
egg yolk	äggula (en)	['ɛg‚ʉːlʲa]

fish	fisk (en)	['fisk]
seafood	fisk och skaldjur	['fisk ɔ 'skalʲjʉːr]
crustaceans	kräftdjur (pl)	['krɛftˌjuːr]
caviar	kaviar (en)	['kavˌjar]

crab	krabba (en)	['kraba]
shrimp	räka (en)	['rɛːka]
oyster	ostron (ett)	['ʊstrʊn]
spiny lobster	languster (en)	[lʲaŋ'gustər]
octopus	bläckfisk (en)	['blʲɛkˌfisk]
squid	bläckfisk (en)	['blʲɛkˌfisk]

sturgeon	stör (en)	['støːr]
salmon	lax (en)	['lʲaks]
halibut	hälleflundra (en)	['hɛlʲeˌflʉndra]

cod	torsk (en)	['tɔːʂk]
mackerel	makrill (en)	['makrilʲ]
tuna	tonfisk (en)	['tʊnˌfisk]
eel	ål (en)	['oːlʲ]

trout	öring (en)	['øːriŋ]
sardine	sardin (en)	[sa'ɟiːn]
pike	gädda (en)	['jɛda]
herring	sill (en)	['silʲ]

bread	bröd (ett)	['brø:d]
cheese	ost (en)	['ʊst]
sugar	socker (ett)	['sɔkər]
salt	salt (ett)	['salʲt]

rice	ris (ett)	['ris]
pasta (macaroni)	pasta (en), makaroner (pl)	['pasta], [maka'rʊnər]
noodles	nudlar (pl)	['nɵ:dlʲar]

butter	smör (ett)	['smœ:r]
vegetable oil	vegetabilisk olja (en)	[vegeta'bilisk 'ɔlja]
sunflower oil	solrosolja (en)	['sʊlʲrʊs,ɔlja]
margarine	margarin (ett)	[marga'rin]

| olives | oliver (pl) | [ʊ:'livər] |
| olive oil | olivolja (en) | [ʊ'liv,ɔlja] |

milk	mjölk (en)	['mjœlʲk]
condensed milk	kondenserad mjölk (en)	[kɔndɛn'serad ,mjœlʲk]
yogurt	yoghurt (en)	['jo:gɵ:t]
sour cream	gräddfil, syrad grädden (en)	['grɛdfilʲ], [syrad 'gredən]
cream (of milk)	grädde (en)	['grɛdə]

| mayonnaise | majonnäs (en) | [majɔ'nɛs] |
| buttercream | kräm (en) | ['krɛm] |

cereal grains (wheat, etc.)	gryn (en)	['gryn]
flour	mjöl (ett)	['mjø:lʲ]
canned food	konserv (en)	[kɔn'sɛrv]

cornflakes	cornflakes (pl)	['kɔ:ɳ,flɛjks]
honey	honung (en)	['hɔnuŋ]
jam	sylt, marmelad (en)	['sylʲt], [marme'lʲad]
chewing gum	tuggummi (ett)	['tug,gumi]

53. Drinks

water	vatten (ett)	['vatən]
drinking water	dricksvatten (ett)	['drɪks,vatən]
mineral water	mineralvatten (ett)	[mine'ralʲ,vatən]

still (adj)	icke kolsyrat	['ikə 'kɔlʲ,syrat]
carbonated (adj)	kolsyrat	['kɔlʲ,syrat]
sparkling (adj)	kolsyrat	['kɔlʲ,syrat]
ice	is (en)	['is]
with ice	med is	[me 'is]
non-alcoholic (adj)	alkoholfri	[alʲkʊ'hɔlʲ,fri:]
soft drink	alkoholfri dryck (en)	[alʲkʊ'hɔlʲfri 'drʏk]

| refreshing drink | läskedryck (en) | ['lɛskə‚drik] |
| lemonade | lemonad (en) | [lʲemɔ'nad] |

liquors	alkoholhaltiga drycker (pl)	[alʲkʊ'hɔlʲ‚halʲtiga 'drʏkər]
wine	vin (ett)	['vin]
white wine	vitvin (ett)	['vit‚vin]
red wine	rödvin (ett)	['rø:d‚vin]

liqueur	likör (en)	[li'kø:r]
champagne	champagne (en)	[ɦam'panʲ]
vermouth	vermouth (en)	['vɛrmut]

whiskey	whisky (en)	['viski]
vodka	vodka (en)	['vodka]
gin	gin (ett)	['dʒin]
cognac	konjak (en)	['konʲak]
rum	rom (en)	['rɔm]

coffee	kaffe (ett)	['kafə]
black coffee	svart kaffe (ett)	['sva:ʈ 'kafə]
coffee with milk	kaffe med mjölk (ett)	['kafə me mjœlʲk]
cappuccino	cappuccino (en)	['kaputʃinʊ]
instant coffee	snabbkaffe (ett)	['snab‚kafə]

milk	mjölk (en)	['mjœlʲk]
cocktail	cocktail (en)	['kɔktɛjlʲ]
milkshake	milkshake (en)	['milʲkʃɛjk]

juice	juice (en)	['ju:s]
tomato juice	tomatjuice (en)	[tʊ'matju:s]
orange juice	apelsinjuice (en)	[apɛlʲ'sinju:s]
freshly squeezed juice	nypressad juice (en)	['nʏ‚prɛsad 'ju:s]

beer	öl (ett)	['ø:lʲ]
light beer	ljust öl (ett)	['jʉ:st‚ø:lʲ]
dark beer	mörkt öl (ett)	['mœ:rkt ‚ø:lʲ]

tea	te (ett)	['te:]
black tea	svart te (ett)	['sva:ʈ ‚te:]
green tea	grönt te (ett)	['grœnt te:]

54. Vegetables

| vegetables | grönsaker (pl) | ['grø:n‚sakər] |
| greens | grönsaker (pl) | ['grø:n‚sakər] |

tomato	tomat (en)	[tʊ'mat]
cucumber	gurka (en)	['gurka]
carrot	morot (en)	['mʊ‚rʊt]

potato	potatis (en)	[pʊ'tatis]
onion	lök (en)	['lʲøːk]
garlic	vitlök (en)	['vit‚lʲøːk]

cabbage	kål (en)	['koːlʲ]
cauliflower	blomkål (en)	['blʲʊm‚koːlʲ]
Brussels sprouts	brysselkål (en)	['brʏsɛlʲ‚koːlʲ]
broccoli	broccoli (en)	['brɔkɔli]

beetroot	rödbeta (en)	['røːd‚beta]
eggplant	aubergine (en)	[ɔbɛr'ʒin]
zucchini	squash, zucchini (en)	['skvɔːɕ], [su'kini]
pumpkin	pumpa (en)	['pumpa]
turnip	rova (en)	['rʊva]

parsley	persilja (en)	[pɛ'ʂilja]
dill	dill (en)	['dilʲ]
lettuce	sallad (en)	['salʲad]
celery	selleri (en)	['sɛlʲeri]
asparagus	sparris (en)	['sparis]
spinach	spenat (en)	[spe'nat]

pea	ärter (pl)	['æːʈər]
beans	bönor (pl)	['bønʊr]
corn (maize)	majs (en)	['majs]
kidney bean	böna (en)	['bøna]

bell pepper	peppar (en)	['pɛpar]
radish	rädisa (en)	['rɛːdisa]
artichoke	kronärtskocka (en)	['krʊnæːʈ‚skɔka]

55. Fruits. Nuts

fruit	frukt (en)	['frʉkt]
apple	äpple (ett)	['ɛplʲe]
pear	päron (ett)	['pæːrɔn]
lemon	citron (en)	[si'trʊn]
orange	apelsin (en)	[apɛlʲ'sin]
strawberry (garden ~)	jordgubbe (en)	['jʊːd‚gubə]

mandarin	mandarin (en)	[manda'rin]
plum	plommon (ett)	['plʲʊmɔn]
peach	persika (en)	['pɛʂika]
apricot	aprikos (en)	[apri'kʊs]
raspberry	hallon (ett)	['halʲɔn]
pineapple	ananas (en)	['ananas]

banana	banan (en)	['banan]
watermelon	vattenmelon (en)	['vatɘn‚me'lʲʉn]
grape	druva (en)	['drʉːva]

sour cherry	körsbär (ett)	['çøːʂˌbæːr]
sweet cherry	fågelbär (ett)	['foːɡəlʲˌbæːr]
melon	melon (en)	[meˈlʲʉn]

grapefruit	grapefrukt (en)	['grɛjpˌfrʉkt]
avocado	avokado (en)	[avɔˈkadʉ]
papaya	papaya (en)	[paˈpaja]
mango	mango (en)	['maŋɡʉ]
pomegranate	granatäpple (en)	[graˈnatˌɛplʲe]

redcurrant	röda vinbär (ett)	['røːda 'vinbæːr]
blackcurrant	svarta vinbär (ett)	['svaːʈa 'vinbæːr]
gooseberry	krusbär (ett)	['krʉːsˌbæːr]
bilberry	blåbär (ett)	['blʲoːˌbæːr]
blackberry	björnbär (ett)	['bjøːɳˌbæːr]

raisin	russin (ett)	['rusin]
fig	fikon (ett)	['fikɔn]
date	dadel (en)	['dadəlʲ]

peanut	jordnöt (en)	['jʉːɖˌnøːt]
almond	mandel (en)	['mandəlʲ]
walnut	valnöt (en)	['valʲˌnøːt]
hazelnut	hasselnöt (en)	['hasəlʲˌnøːt]
coconut	kokosnöt (en)	['kʉkʉsˌnøːt]
pistachios	pistaschnötter (pl)	['pistaʃˌnœtər]

56. Bread. Candy

bakers' confectionery (pastry)	konditorivaror (pl)	[kɔndituˈriːˌvarʉr]
bread	bröd (ett)	['brøːd]
cookies	småkakor (pl)	['smoːkakʉr]

chocolate (n)	choklad (en)	[ʃɔkˈlʲad]
chocolate (as adj)	choklad-	[ʃɔkˈlʲad-]
candy (wrapped)	konfekt, karamell (en)	[kɔnˈfɛkt], [karaˈmɛlʲ]

| cake (e.g., cupcake) | kaka, bakelse (en) | ['kaka], ['bakəlʲsə] |
| cake (e.g., birthday ~) | tårta (en) | ['toːʈa] |

| pie (e.g., apple ~) | paj (en) | ['paj] |
| filling (for cake, pie) | fyllning (en) | ['fylʲniŋ] |

| jam (whole fruit jam) | sylt (en) | ['sylʲt] |
| marmalade | marmelad (en) | [marmeˈlʲad] |

waffles	våffle (en)	['vɔflʲe]
ice-cream	glass (en)	['glʲas]
pudding	pudding (en)	['pudiŋ]

57. Spices

salt	salt (ett)	['salit]
salty (adj)	salt	['salit]
to salt (vt)	att salta	[at 'salita]

black pepper	svartpeppar (en)	['sva:t̯pɛpar]
red pepper (milled ~)	rödpeppar (en)	['rø:d̯pɛpar]
mustard	senap (en)	['se:nap]
horseradish	pepparrot (en)	['pɛpa̯rʊt]

condiment	krydda (en)	['krʏda]
spice	krydda (en)	['krʏda]
sauce	sås (en)	['so:s]
vinegar	ättika (en)	['ætika]

anise	anis (en)	['anis]
basil	basilika (en)	[ba'silika]
cloves	nejlika (en)	['nɛjlika]
ginger	ingefära (en)	['iŋə̯fæ:ra]
coriander	koriander (en)	[kɔri'andər]
cinnamon	kanel (en)	[ka'neli]

sesame	sesam (en)	['sesam]
bay leaf	lagerblad (ett)	['liagə̯r̩bliad]
paprika	paprika (en)	['paprika]
caraway	kummin (en)	['kumin]
saffron	saffran (en)	['safran]

PERSONAL INFORMATION. FAMILY

58. Personal information. Forms

name (first name)	namn (ett)	['namn]
surname (last name)	efternamn (ett)	['ɛftə‚ŋamn]
date of birth	födelsedatum (ett)	['føːdəlˈsə‚datum]
place of birth	födelseort (en)	['føːdəlˈsə‚ɔːt]
nationality	nationalitet (en)	[natɧunaliˈtet]
place of residence	bostadsort (en)	['bostads‚ɔːt]
country	land (ett)	['lˈand]
profession (occupation)	yrke (ett),	['yrkə],
	profession (en)	[profeˈɧun]
gender, sex	kön (ett)	['ɕøːn]
height	höjd (en)	['hœjd]
weight	vikt (en)	['vikt]

59. Family members. Relatives

mother	mor (en)	['mʊr]
father	far (en)	['far]
son	son (en)	['sɔn]
daughter	dotter (en)	['dɔtər]
younger daughter	yngsta dotter (en)	['yŋsta 'dɔtər]
younger son	yngste son (en)	['yŋstə sɔn]
eldest daughter	äldsta dotter (en)	['ɛlˈsta 'dɔtər]
eldest son	äldste son (en)	['ɛlˈstə 'sɔn]
brother	bror (en)	['brʊr]
elder brother	storebror (en)	['stʊrə‚brʊr]
younger brother	lillebror (en)	['lilˈe‚brʊr]
sister	syster (en)	['systər]
elder sister	storasyster (en)	['stʊra‚systər]
younger sister	lillasyster (en)	['lilˈa‚systər]
cousin (masc.)	kusin (en)	[kʉˈsiːn]
cousin (fem.)	kusin (en)	[kʉˈsiːn]
mom, mommy	mamma (en)	['mama]
dad, daddy	pappa (en)	['papa]
parents	föräldrar (pl)	[førˈɛlˈdrar]
child	barn (ett)	['baːŋ]

children	barn (pl)	['ba:n]
grandmother	mormor, farmor (en)	['murmur], ['farmur]
grandfather	morfar, farfar (en)	['murfar], ['farfar]
grandson	barnbarn (ett)	['ba:n‚ba:n]
granddaughter	barnbarn (ett)	['ba:n‚ba:n]
grandchildren	barnbarn (pl)	['ba:n‚ba:n]

uncle	farbror, morbror (en)	['far‚brur], ['mur‚brur]
aunt	faster, moster (en)	['fastər], ['mustər]
nephew	brorson, systerson (en)	['brur‚sɔn], ['systə‚sɔn]
niece	brorsdotter, systerdotter (en)	['bru:s‚dɔtər], ['systə‚dɔtər]

mother-in-law (wife's mother)	svärmor (en)	['svæ:r‚mur]
father-in-law (husband's father)	svärfar (en)	['svæ:r‚far]
son-in-law (daughter's husband)	svärson (en)	['svæ:‚sɔn]

stepmother	styvmor (en)	['styv‚mur]
stepfather	styvfar (en)	['styv‚far]

infant	spädbarn (ett)	['spɛ:d‚ba:n]
baby (infant)	spädbarn (ett)	['spɛ:d‚ba:n]
little boy, kid	baby, bäbis (en)	['bɛ:bi], ['bɛ:bis]

wife	hustru (en)	['hʉstrʉ]
husband	man (en)	['man]

spouse (husband)	make, äkta make (en)	['makə], ['ɛkta ‚makə]
spouse (wife)	hustru (en)	['hʉstrʉ]

married (masc.)	gift	['jift]
married (fem.)	gift	['jift]
single (unmarried)	ogift	[ʊ:'jift]
bachelor	ungkarl (en)	['uŋ‚kar]
divorced (masc.)	frånskild	['fro:n‚ɧilᵈd]

widow	änka (en)	['ɛŋka]
widower	änkling (en)	['ɛŋkliŋ]

relative	släkting (en)	['slᶥɛktiŋ]
close relative	nära släkting (en)	['næ:ra 'slᶥɛktiŋ]

distant relative	fjärran släkting (en)	['fjæ:ran 'slᶥɛktiŋ]
relatives	släktingar (pl)	['slᶥɛktiŋar]

orphan (boy or girl)	föräldralöst barn (ett)	[før'ɛlᶥdralᶥœst 'ba:n]
guardian (of a minor)	förmyndare (en)	['før‚myndarə]
to adopt (a boy)	att adoptera	[at adɔp'tera]
to adopt (a girl)	att adoptera	[at adɔp'tera]

60. Friends. Coworkers

friend (masc.)	vän (en)	['vɛ:n]
friend (fem.)	väninna (en)	[vɛ:'nina]
friendship	vänskap (en)	['vɛn‚skap]
to be friends	att vara vänner	[at 'vara 'vɛnər]
buddy (masc.)	vän (en)	['vɛ:n]
buddy (fem.)	väninna (en)	[vɛ:'nina]
partner	partner (en)	['pa:ʈnər]
chief (boss)	chef (en)	['ɧef]
superior (n)	överordnad (en)	['ø:vər‚ɔ:ɖnat]
owner, proprietor	ägare (en)	['ɛ:garə]
subordinate (n)	underordnad (en)	['undər‚ɔ:ɖnat]
colleague	kollega (en)	[kɔ'lʲe:ga]
acquaintance (person)	bekant (en)	[be'kant]
fellow traveler	resekamrat (en)	['resə‚kam'rat]
classmate	klasskamrat (en)	['klʲas‚kam'rat]
neighbor (masc.)	granne (en)	['granə]
neighbor (fem.)	granne (en)	['granə]
neighbors	grannar (pl)	['granar]

HUMAN BODY. MEDICINE

61. Head

head	huvud (ett)	['hʉ:vʉd]
face	ansikte (ett)	['ansiktə]
nose	näsa (en)	['nɛ:sa]
mouth	mun (en)	['mu:n]
eye	öga (ett)	['ø:ga]
eyes	ögon (pl)	['ø:gɔn]
pupil	pupill (en)	[pʉ'pilʲ]
eyebrow	ögonbryn (ett)	['ø:gɔn͵bryn]
eyelash	ögonfrans (en)	['ø:gɔn͵frans]
eyelid	ögonlock (ett)	['ø:gɔn͵lʲɔk]
tongue	tunga (en)	['tuŋa]
tooth	tand (en)	['tand]
lips	läppar (pl)	['lʲɛpar]
cheekbones	kindben (pl)	['çind͵be:n]
gum	tandkött (ett)	['tand͵çœt]
palate	gom (en)	['gʊm]
nostrils	näsborrar (pl)	['nɛ:s͵bɔrar]
chin	haka (en)	['haka]
jaw	käke (en)	['çɛ:kə]
cheek	kind (en)	['çind]
forehead	panna (en)	['pana]
temple	tinning (en)	['tiniŋ]
ear	öra (ett)	['ø:ra]
back of the head	nacke (en)	['nakə]
neck	hals (en)	['halʲs]
throat	strupe, hals (en)	['strʉpə], ['halʲs]
hair	hår (pl)	['ho:r]
hairstyle	frisyr (en)	[fri'syr]
haircut	klippning (en)	['klipniŋ]
wig	peruk (en)	[pe'rʉ:k]
mustache	mustasch (en)	[mʉ'sta:ʃ]
beard	skägg (ett)	['ʃɛg]
to have (a beard, etc.)	att ha	[at 'ha]
braid	fläta (en)	['flʲɛ:ta]
sideburns	polisonger (pl)	[pɔli'sɔŋər]
red-haired (adj)	rödhårig	['rø:d͵ho:rig]

gray (hair)	grå	['gro:]
bald (adj)	skallig	['skalig]
bald patch	flint (en)	['flint]

| ponytail | hästsvans (en) | ['hɛst‚svans] |
| bangs | lugg, pannlugg (en) | [lʉg], ['pan‚lʉg] |

62. Human body

| hand | hand (en) | ['hand] |
| arm | arm (en) | ['arm] |

finger	finger (ett)	['fiŋər]
toe	tå (en)	['to:]
thumb	tumme (en)	['tumə]
little finger	lillfinger (ett)	['lilʲ‚fiŋər]
nail	nagel (en)	['nagəlʲ]

fist	knytnäve (en)	['knʏt‚nɛ:və]
palm	handflata (en)	['hand‚flʲata]
wrist	handled (en)	['hand‚lʲed]
forearm	underarm (en)	['undər‚arm]
elbow	armbåge (en)	['arm‚bo:gə]
shoulder	skuldra (en)	['skʉlʲdra]

leg	ben (ett)	['be:n]
foot	fot (en)	['fʊt]
knee	knä (ett)	['knɛ:]
calf (part of leg)	vad (ett)	['vad]
hip	höft (en)	['hœft]
heel	häl (en)	['hɛ:lʲ]

body	kropp (en)	['krɔp]
stomach	mage (en)	['magə]
chest	bröst (ett)	['brœst]
breast	bröst (ett)	['brœst]
flank	sida (en)	['sida]
back	rygg (en)	['rʏg]
lower back	ländrygg (en)	['lʲɛnd‚rʏg]
waist	midja (en)	['midja]

navel (belly button)	navel (en)	['navəlʲ]
buttocks	stjärtar, skinkor (pl)	['ɧæ:‚ʈar], ['ɧiŋkʊr]
bottom	bak (en)	['bak]

beauty mark	leverfläck (ett)	['lʲevər‚flɛk]
birthmark	födelsemärke (ett)	['fø:dəlʲsə‚mæ:rkə]
(café au lait spot)		
tattoo	tatuering (en)	[tatʉ'eriŋ]
scar	ärr (ett)	['ær]

63. Diseases

sickness	sjukdom (en)	['ɧʉːkˌdʊm]
to be sick	att vara sjuk	[at 'vara 'ɧʉːk]
health	hälsa, sundhet (en)	['hɛlˈsa], ['sundˌhet]

runny nose (coryza)	snuva (en)	['snʉːva]
tonsillitis	halsfluss, angina (en)	['halˈsˌflʉs], [aŋ'gina]
cold (illness)	förkylning (en)	[før'ɕylˈniŋ]
to catch a cold	att bli förkyld	[at bli før'ɕylˈd]

bronchitis	bronkit (en)	[broŋ'kit]
pneumonia	lunginflammation (en)	['lʉŋˌinflˈamaˈfɧʊn]
flu, influenza	influensa (en)	[inflʉ'ɛnsa]

nearsighted (adj)	närsynt	['næːˌsʏnt]
farsighted (adj)	långsynt	['lˈɔŋˌsʏnt]
strabismus (crossed eyes)	skelögdhet (en)	['ɧelˈøgdˌhet]
cross-eyed (adj)	skelögd	['ɧelˈˌøgd]
cataract	grå starr (en)	['gro: 'star]
glaucoma	grön starr (en)	['grøːn 'star]

stroke	stroke (en), hjärnslag (ett)	['stroːk], ['jæːnˌslˈag]
heart attack	infarkt (en)	[in'farkt]
myocardial infarction	hjärtinfarkt (en)	['jæːt in'farkt]
paralysis	förlamning (en)	[fœ:'lˈamniŋ]
to paralyze (vt)	att förlama	[at fœ:'lˈama]

allergy	allergi (en)	[alˈer'gi]
asthma	astma (en)	['astma]
diabetes	diabetes (en)	[dia'betəs]

toothache	tandvärk (en)	['tandˌvæːrk]
caries	karies (en)	['karies]

diarrhea	diarré (en)	[dia're:]
constipation	förstoppning (en)	[fœ:'ʂtopniŋ]
stomach upset	magbesvär (ett)	['magˌbe'svɛ:r]
food poisoning	matförgiftning (en)	['matˌfør'jiftniŋ]
to get food poisoning	att få matförgiftning	[at fo: 'matˌfør'jiftniŋ]

arthritis	artrit (en)	[a'trit]
rickets	rakitis (en)	[ra'kitis]
rheumatism	reumatism (en)	[revma'tism]
atherosclerosis	åderförkalkning (en)	['o:dɛrførˌkalˈkniŋ]

gastritis	gastrit (en)	[ga'strit]
appendicitis	appendicit (en)	[apɛndi'sit]
cholecystitis	cholecystit (en)	[holəsys'tit]
ulcer	magsår (ett)	['magˌso:r]

measles	mässling (en)	['mɛs,liŋ]
rubella (German measles)	röda hund (en)	['rø:da 'hund]
jaundice	gulsot (en)	['gʉːlʲ,sʊt]
hepatitis	hepatit (en)	[hepa'tit]

schizophrenia	schizofreni (en)	[skitsɔfre'ni:]
rabies (hydrophobia)	rabies (en)	['rabies]
neurosis	neuros (en)	[nev'rɔs]
concussion	hjärnskakning (en)	['jæː.nˌskakniŋ]

cancer	cancer (en)	['kansər]
sclerosis	skleros (en)	[sklʲe'rɔs]
multiple sclerosis	multipel skleros (en)	[mʉlʲ'tipəlʲ sklʲe'rɔs]

alcoholism	alkoholism (en)	[alʲkʊhɔ'lizm]
alcoholic (n)	alkoholist (en)	[alʲkʊhɔ'list]
syphilis	syfilis (en)	['syfilis]
AIDS	AIDS	['ɛjds]

tumor	tumör (en)	[tʉ'møːr]
malignant (adj)	elakartad	['ɛlʲak,aːʈad]
benign (adj)	godartad	['gʊd,aːʈad]

fever	feber (en)	['febər]
malaria	malaria (en)	[ma'lʲaria]
gangrene	kallbrand (en)	['kalʲˌbrand]
seasickness	sjösjuka (en)	['ɧøːˌɧʉːka]
epilepsy	epilepsi (en)	[epilʲep'siː]

epidemic	epidemi (en)	[ɛpide'miː]
typhus	tyfus (en)	['tyfʉs]
tuberculosis	tuberkulos (en)	[tʉbɛrkʉ'lʲɔs]
cholera	kolera (en)	['kʊlʲera]
plague (bubonic ~)	pest (en)	['pɛst]

64. Symptoms. Treatments. Part 1

symptom	symptom (ett)	[sʏmp'tɔm]
temperature	temperatur (en)	[tɛmpəra'tʉːr]
high temperature (fever)	hög temperatur (en)	['høːg tɛmpəra'tʉːr]
pulse	puls (en)	['pulʲs]

dizziness (vertigo)	yrsel, svindel (en)	['yːʂəlʲ], ['svindəlʲ]
hot (adj)	varm	['varm]
shivering	rysning (en)	['rʏsniŋ]
pale (e.g., ~ face)	blek	['blʲek]

cough	hosta (en)	['hʊsta]
to cough (vi)	att hosta	[at 'hʊsta]
to sneeze (vi)	att nysa	[at 'nysa]

| faint | svimning (en) | ['svimniŋ] |
| to faint (vi) | att svimma | [at 'svima] |

bruise (hématome)	blåmärke (ett)	['blˈoːˌmæːrkə]
bump (lump)	bula (en)	['bʉːlˈa]
to bang (bump)	att slå sig	[at 'slˈoː sɛj]
contusion (bruise)	blåmärke (ett)	['blˈoːˌmæːrkə]
to get a bruise	att slå sig	[at 'slˈoː sɛj]

to limp (vi)	att halta	[at 'halˈta]
dislocation	vrickning (en)	['vrikniŋ]
to dislocate (vt)	att förvrida	[at før'vrida]
fracture	brott (ett), fraktur (en)	['brɔt], [frak'tʉːr]
to have a fracture	att få en fraktur	[at fo: en frak'tʉːr]

cut (e.g., paper ~)	skärsår (ett)	['ɧæːˌsoːr]
to cut oneself	att skära sig	[at 'ɧæːra sɛj]
bleeding	blödning (en)	['blˈœdniŋ]

| burn (injury) | brännsår (ett) | ['brɛnˌsoːr] |
| to get burned | att bränna sig | [at 'brɛna sɛj] |

to prick (vt)	att sticka	[at 'stika]
to prick oneself	att sticka sig	[at 'stika sɛj]
to injure (vt)	att skada	[at 'skada]
injury	skada (en)	['skada]
wound	sår (ett)	['soːr]
trauma	trauma (en)	['travma]

to be delirious	att tala i feberyra	[at 'talˈa i 'febəryra]
to stutter (vi)	att stamma	[at 'stama]
sunstroke	solsting (ett)	['sʉlˈˌstiŋ]

65. Symptoms. Treatments. Part 2

| pain, ache | värk, smärta (en) | ['væːrk], ['smɛʈa] |
| splinter (in foot, etc.) | sticka (en) | ['stika] |

sweat (perspiration)	svett (en)	['svɛt]
to sweat (perspire)	att svettas	[at 'svɛtas]
vomiting	kräkning (en)	['krɛkniŋ]
convulsions	kramper (pl)	['krampər]

pregnant (adj)	gravid	[gra'vid]
to be born	att födas	[at 'føːdas]
delivery, labor	förlossning (en)	[fœːˈʟˈosniŋ]
to deliver (~ a baby)	att föda	[at 'føːda]
abortion	abort (en)	[a'bɔːt]
breathing, respiration	andning (en)	['andniŋ]
in-breath (inhalation)	inandning (en)	['inˌandniŋ]

out-breath (exhalation)	utandning (en)	['ʉt͵andniŋ]
to exhale (breathe out)	att andas ut	[at 'andas ʉt]
to inhale (vi)	att andas in	[at 'andas in]

disabled person	handikappad person (en)	['handi͵kapad pɛ'ʂʉn]
cripple	krympling (en)	['krʏmpliŋ]
drug addict	narkoman (en)	[narkʉ'man]

deaf (adj)	döv	['dø:v]
mute (adj)	stum	['stu:m]
deaf mute (adj)	dövstum	['dø:v͵stu:m]

mad, insane (adj)	mentalsjuk, galen	['mental'ɧʉ:k], ['galʲen]
madman	dåre, galning (en)	['do:rə], ['galʲniŋ]
(demented person)		
madwoman	dåre, galning (en)	['do:rə], ['galʲniŋ]
to go insane	att bli sinnessjuk	[at bli 'sinɛs͵ɧʉ:k]

gene	gen (en)	['jen]
immunity	immunitet (en)	[imʉni'te:t]
hereditary (adj)	ärftlig	['æ:rftlig]
congenital (adj)	medfödd	['med͵fœd]

virus	virus (ett)	['vi:rʉs]
microbe	mikrob (en)	[mi'krɔb]
bacterium	bakterie (en)	[bak'teriə]
infection	infektion (en)	[infɛk'ɧʊn]

66. Symptoms. Treatments. Part 3

| hospital | sjukhus (ett) | ['ɧʉ:k͵hʉs] |
| patient | patient (en) | [pasi'ent] |

diagnosis	diagnos (en)	[dia'gnɔs]
cure	kur (en)	['kʉ:r]
medical treatment	behandling (en)	[be'handliŋ]
to get treatment	att bli behandlad	[at bli be'handlʲad]
to treat (~ a patient)	att behandla	[at be'handlʲa]
to nurse (look after)	att sköta	[at 'ɧø:ta]
care (nursing ~)	vård (en)	['vo:ɖ]

operation, surgery	operation (en)	[ɔpera'ɧʊn]
to bandage (head, limb)	att förbinda	[at før'binda]
bandaging	förbindning (en)	[før'bindniŋ]

vaccination	vaccination (en)	[vaksina'ɧʊn]
to vaccinate (vt)	att vaksinera	[at vaksi'nera]
injection, shot	injektion (en)	[injɛk'ɧʊn]
to give an injection	att ge en spruta	[at je: en 'sprʉta]
attack	anfall (ett), attack (en)	['anfalʲ], [a'tak]

amputation	amputation (en)	[ampɵta'hɵn]
to amputate (vt)	att amputera	[at ampɵ'tera]
coma	koma (ett)	['kɔma]
to be in a coma	att ligga i koma	[at 'liga i 'kɔma]
intensive care	intensivavdelning (en)	[intɛn'siv‚av'dɛlˡniŋ]

to recover (~ from flu)	att återhämta sig	[at 'oːter‚hɛmta sɛj]
condition (patient's ~)	tillstånd (ett)	['tilˡ‚stɔnd]
consciousness	medvetande (ett)	['med‚vetandə]
memory (faculty)	minne (ett)	['minə]

to pull out (tooth)	att dra ut	[at 'dra ɵt]
filling	plomb (en)	['plˡɔmb]
to fill (a tooth)	att plombera	[at plˡɔm'bera]

| hypnosis | hypnos (en) | [hɵp'nɔs] |
| to hypnotize (vt) | att hypnotisera | [at 'hɵpnɔti‚sera] |

67. Medicine. Drugs. Accessories

medicine, drug	medicin (en)	[medi'sin]
remedy	medel (ett)	['medəlˡ]
to prescribe (vt)	att ordinera	[at oːdi'nera]
prescription	recept (ett)	[re'sɛpt]

tablet, pill	tablett (en)	[tab'lˡet]
ointment	salva (en)	['salˡva]
ampule	ampull (en)	[am'pulˡ]
mixture	mixtur (en)	[miks'tɵːr]
syrup	sirap (en)	['sirap]
pill	piller (ett)	['pilˡer]
powder	pulver (ett)	['pulˡvər]

gauze bandage	gasbinda (en)	['gas‚binda]
cotton wool	vadd (en)	['vad]
iodine	jod (en)	['jɵd]
Band-Aid	plåster (ett)	['plˡɔstər]
eyedropper	pipett (en)	[pi'pɛt]
thermometer	termometer (en)	[tɛrmɵ'metər]
syringe	spruta (en)	['sprɵta]

| wheelchair | rullstol (en) | ['rɵlˡ‚stɵlˡ] |
| crutches | kryckor (pl) | ['krɵkɵr] |

painkiller	smärtstillande medel (ett)	['smæːt‚stilˡande 'medəlˡ]
laxative	laxermedel (ett)	['lˡaksər 'medəlˡ]
spirits (ethanol)	sprit (en)	['sprit]
medicinal herbs	läkeväxter (pl)	['lˡɛkə‚vɛkstər]
herbal (~ tea)	ört-	['øːt-]

APARTMENT

68. Apartment

apartment	lägenhet (en)	['lʲeːgənˌhet]
room	rum (ett)	['ruːm]
bedroom	sovrum (ett)	['sɔvˌrum]
dining room	matsal (en)	['matsalʲ]
living room	vardagsrum (ett)	['vaːdasˌrum]
study (home office)	arbetsrum (ett)	['arbetsˌrum]
entry room	entréhall (en)	[ɛntreːhalʲ]
bathroom (room with a bath or shower)	badrum (ett)	['badˌruːm]
half bath	toalett (en)	[tʊa'lʲet]
ceiling	tak (ett)	['tak]
floor	golv (ett)	['gɔlʲv]
corner	hörn (ett)	['høːŋ]

69. Furniture. Interior

furniture	möbel (en)	['møːbəlʲ]
table	bord (ett)	['buːd]
chair	stol (en)	['stʊlʲ]
bed	säng (en)	['sɛŋ]
couch, sofa	soffa (en)	['sɔfa]
armchair	fåtölj, länstol (en)	[foː'tœlj], ['lɛnˌstʊlʲ]
bookcase	bokhylla (en)	['bʊkˌhylʲa]
shelf	hylla (en)	['hylʲa]
wardrobe	garderob (en)	[gaːdə'rɔːb]
coat rack (wall-mounted ~)	knagg (en)	['knag]
coat stand	klädhängare (en)	['klʲɛdˌhɛŋarə]
bureau, dresser	byrå (en)	['byrɔː]
coffee table	soffbord (ett)	['sɔfˌbuːd]
mirror	spegel (en)	['spegəlʲ]
carpet	matta (en)	['mata]
rug, small carpet	liten matta (en)	['litən 'mata]
fireplace	kamin (en), eldstad (ett)	[ka'min], ['ɛlʲdˌstad]
candle	ljus (ett)	['jʉːs]

candlestick	ljusstake (en)	['jʉːsˌstakə]
drapes	gardiner (pl)	[ga:'dinər]
wallpaper	tapet (en)	[ta'pet]
blinds (jalousie)	persienn (en)	[pɛ'sjen]

table lamp	bordslampa (en)	['buːds̩ˌlʲampa]
wall lamp (sconce)	vägglampa (en)	['vɛgˌlʲampa]
floor lamp	golvlampa (en)	['gɔlʲvˌlʲampa]
chandelier	ljuskrona (en)	['jʉːsˌkrʊna]

leg (of chair, table)	ben (ett)	['beːn]
armrest	armstöd (ett)	['armˌstøːd]
back (backrest)	rygg (en)	['rɤg]
drawer	låda (en)	['lʲoːda]

70. Bedding

bedclothes	sängkläder (pl)	['sɛŋˌklʲɛːdər]
pillow	kudde (en)	['kudə]
pillowcase	örngott (ett)	['øːrɳˌgɔt]
duvet, comforter	duntäcke (ett)	['dʉːnˌtɛkə]
sheet	lakan (ett)	['lʲakan]
bedspread	överkast (ett)	['øːvəˌkast]

71. Kitchen

kitchen	kök (ett)	['ɕøːk]
gas	gas (en)	['gas]
gas stove (range)	gasspis (en)	['gasˌspis]
electric stove	elektrisk spis (en)	[ɛ'lʲektrisk ˌspis]
oven	bakugn (en)	['bakˌugn]
microwave oven	mikrovågsugn (en)	['mikrʊvɔgsˌugn]

refrigerator	kylskåp (ett)	['ɕylʲˌskoːp]
freezer	frys (en)	['frys]
dishwasher	diskmaskin (en)	['diskˌma'fiːn]

meat grinder	köttkvarn (en)	['ɕœtˌkvaːɳ]
juicer	juicepress (en)	['juːsˌprɛs]
toaster	brödrost (en)	['brøːdˌrɔst]
mixer	mixer (en)	['miksər]

coffee machine	kaffebryggare (en)	['kafəˌbrɤgarə]
coffee pot	kaffekanna (en)	['kafəˌkana]
coffee grinder	kaffekvarn (en)	['kafəˌkvaːɳ]

| kettle | tekittel (en) | ['teˌɕitəlʲ] |
| teapot | tekanna (en) | ['teˌkana] |

lid	**lock (ett)**	['lɔk]
tea strainer	**tesil (en)**	['teˌsilʲ]
spoon	**sked (en)**	['ɧed]
teaspoon	**tesked (en)**	['teˌɧed]
soup spoon	**matsked (en)**	['matˌɧed]
fork	**gaffel (en)**	['gafəlʲ]
knife	**kniv (en)**	['kniv]
tableware (dishes)	**servis (en)**	[sɛr'vis]
plate (dinner ~)	**tallrik (en)**	['talʲrik]
saucer	**tefat (ett)**	['teˌfat]
shot glass	**shotglas (ett)**	['ʃotˌglʲas]
glass (tumbler)	**glas (ett)**	['glʲas]
cup	**kopp (en)**	['kɔp]
sugar bowl	**sockerskål (en)**	['sɔkə:ˌsko:lʲ]
salt shaker	**saltskål (en)**	['salʲtˌsko:lʲ]
pepper shaker	**pepparskål (en)**	['pɛpaˌsko:lʲ]
butter dish	**smörfat (en)**	['smœrˌfat]
stock pot (soup pot)	**kastrull, gryta (en)**	[ka'strulʲ], ['gryta]
frying pan (skillet)	**stekpanna (en)**	['stekˌpana]
ladle	**slev (en)**	['slʲev]
colander	**durkslag (ett)**	['durkˌslʲag]
tray (serving ~)	**bricka (en)**	['brika]
bottle	**flaska (en)**	['flʲaska]
jar (glass)	**glasburk (en)**	['glʲasˌburk]
can	**burk (en)**	['burk]
bottle opener	**flasköppnare (en)**	['flʲaskˌøpnarə]
can opener	**burköppnare (en)**	['burkˌøpnarə]
corkscrew	**korkskruv (en)**	['kɔrkˌskrʉ:v]
filter	**filter (ett)**	['filʲtər]
to filter (vt)	**att filtrera**	[at filʲ'trera]
trash, garbage (food waste, etc.)	**sopor, avfall (ett)**	['supʊr], ['avfalʲ]
trash can (kitchen ~)	**sophink (en)**	['supˌhiŋk]

72. Bathroom

bathroom	**badrum (ett)**	['badˌru:m]
water	**vatten (ett)**	['vatən]
faucet	**kran (en)**	['kran]
hot water	**varmvatten (ett)**	['varmˌvatən]
cold water	**kallvatten (ett)**	['kalʲˌvatən]
toothpaste	**tandkräm (en)**	['tandˌkrɛm]

| to brush one's teeth | att borsta tänderna | [at 'bɔːʂta 'tɛndɛːŋa] |
| toothbrush | tandborste (en) | ['tand͵bɔːʂtə] |

to shave (vi)	att raka sig	[at 'raka sɛj]
shaving foam	raklödder (ett)	['rak͵lʲødər]
razor	hyvel (en)	['hyvəlʲ]

to wash (one's hands, etc.)	att tvätta	[at 'tvæta]
to take a bath	att tvätta sig	[at 'tvæta sɛj]
shower	dusch (en)	['duʃ]
to take a shower	att duscha	[at 'duʃa]

bathtub	badkar (ett)	['bad͵kar]
toilet (toilet bowl)	toalettstol (en)	[tʊa'lʲet͵stʊlʲ]
sink (washbasin)	handfat (ett)	['hand͵fat]

| soap | tvål (en) | ['tvoːlʲ] |
| soap dish | tvålskål (en) | ['tvoːlʲ͵skoːlʲ] |

sponge	svamp (en)	['svamp]
shampoo	schampo (ett)	['ʃam͵pʊ]
towel	handduk (en)	['hand͵dɯːk]
bathrobe	morgonrock (en)	['mɔrgɔn͵rɔk]

laundry (process)	tvätt (en)	['tvæt]
washing machine	tvättmaskin (en)	['tvæt͵ma'ʃiːn]
to do the laundry	att tvätta kläder	[at 'tvæta 'klʲɛːdər]
laundry detergent	tvättmedel (ett)	['tvæt͵medəlʲ]

73. Household appliances

TV set	teve (en)	['teve]
tape recorder	bandspelare (en)	['band͵spelʲarə]
VCR (video recorder)	video (en)	['videʊ]
radio	radio (en)	['radiʊ]
player (CD, MP3, etc.)	spelare (en)	['spelʲarə]

video projector	videoprojektor (en)	['videʊ prʊ'jɛktʊr]
home movie theater	hemmabio (en)	['hɛma͵biːʊ]
DVD player	DVD spelare (en)	[deve'de: ͵spelʲarə]
amplifier	förstärkare (en)	[fœː'ʂtæːkarə]
video game console	spelkonsol (en)	['spelʲ kɔn'sɔlʲ]

video camera	videokamera (en)	['videʊ͵kamera]
camera (photo)	kamera (en)	['kamera]
digital camera	digitalkamera (en)	[digi'talʲ ͵kamera]

vacuum cleaner	dammsugare (en)	['dam͵sɯgarə]
iron (e.g., steam ~)	strykjärn (ett)	['stryk͵jæːɳ]
ironing board	strykbräda (en)	['stryk͵brɛːda]

telephone	telefon (en)	[tel'e'fɔn]
cell phone	mobiltelefon (en)	[mɔ'bil' tel'e'fɔn]
typewriter	skrivmaskin (en)	['skriv‚ma'ɧi:n]
sewing machine	symaskin (en)	['sy‚ma'ɧi:n]

microphone	mikrofon (en)	[mikrʊ'fɔn]
headphones	hörlurar (pl)	['hœ:‚l'ʉ:rar]
remote control (TV)	fjärrkontroll (en)	['fjæ:r‚kɔn'trol']

CD, compact disc	cd-skiva (en)	['sede ‚ɧiva]
cassette, tape	kassett (en)	[ka'sɛt]
vinyl record	skiva (en)	['ɧiva]

THE EARTH. WEATHER

74. Outer space

space	rymden, kosmos (ett)	[rʏmden], ['kɔsmɔs]
space (as adj)	rymd-	['rʏmd-]
outer space	yttre rymd (en)	['ytrə ˌrʏmd]
world	värld (en)	['væːd]
universe	universum (ett)	[uni'vɛːʂum]
galaxy	galax (en)	[ga'lʲaks]
star	stjärna (en)	['ɧæːɳa]
constellation	stjärnbild (en)	['ɧæːɳˌbilʲd]
planet	planet (en)	[plʲa'net]
satellite	satellit (en)	[satɛ'liːt]
meteorite	meteorit (en)	[meteʊ'rit]
comet	komet (en)	[kʊ'met]
asteroid	asteroid (en)	[asterʊ'id]
orbit	bana (en)	['bana]
to revolve (~ around the Earth)	att rotera	[at rʊ'tera]
atmosphere	atmosfär (en)	[atmʊ'sfæːr]
the Sun	Solen	['sʊlʲən]
solar system	solsystem (ett)	['sʊlʲ ˌsʏ'stem]
solar eclipse	solförmörkelse (en)	['sʊlʲfør'mœːrkəlʲsə]
the Earth	Jorden	['jʊːdən]
the Moon	Månen	['moːnən]
Mars	Mars	['maːʂ]
Venus	Venus	['veːnus]
Jupiter	Jupiter	['jupitər]
Saturn	Saturnus	[sa'tuːɳus]
Mercury	Merkurius	[mɛr'kurius]
Uranus	Uranus	[ʉ'ranus]
Neptune	Neptunus	[nep'tʉnus]
Pluto	Pluto	['plʉtʊ]
Milky Way	Vintergatan	['vintəˌgatan]
Great Bear (Ursa Major)	Stora bjornen	['stʊra 'bjʊːɳən]
North Star	Polstjärnan	['pʊlʲˌɧæːɳan]
Martian	marsian (en)	[maːʂi'an]

extraterrestrial (n)	utomjording (en)	['ʉtɔmˌjʉːɖisk]
alien	rymdväsen (ett)	['rʏmdˌvɛsən]
flying saucer	flygande tefat (ett)	['flʲygandə 'tefat]

spaceship	rymdskepp (ett)	['rʏmdˌɧɛp]
space station	rymdstation (en)	['rʏmd staˈɧʊn]
blast-off	start (en)	['staːt]

engine	motor (en)	['mʊtʊr]
nozzle	dysa (en)	['dysa]
fuel	bränsle (ett)	['brɛnslʲe]

cockpit, flight deck	cockpit, flygdäck (en)	['kɔkpit], ['flʏgˌdɛk]
antenna	antenn (en)	[anˈtɛn]
porthole	fönster (ett)	['fœnstər]
solar panel	solbatteri (ett)	['sʊlʲˌbatɛˈriː]
spacesuit	rymddräkt (en)	['rʏmdˌdrɛkt]

| weightlessness | tyngdlöshet (en) | ['tʏŋdlʲøsˌhet] |
| oxygen | syre, oxygen (ett) | ['syrə], ['oksygən] |

| docking (in space) | dockning (en) | ['dɔkniŋ] |
| to dock (vi, vt) | att docka | [at 'dɔka] |

observatory	observatorium (ett)	[ɔbsɛrvaˈtʊrium]
telescope	teleskop (ett)	[telʲeˈskɔp]
to observe (vt)	att observera	[at ɔbsɛrˈvera]
to explore (vt)	att utforska	[at 'ʉtˌfɔːʂka]

75. The Earth

the Earth	Jorden	['jʊːɖən]
the globe (the Earth)	jordklot (ett)	['jʊːɖˌklʲʊt]
planet	planet (en)	[plʲaˈnet]

atmosphere	atmosfär (en)	[atmʊˈsfæːr]
geography	geografi (en)	[jeʊgraˈfiː]
nature	natur (en)	[naˈtʉːr]

globe (table ~)	glob (en)	['glʲʊb]
map	karta (en)	['kaːʈa]
atlas	atlas (en)	['atlʲas]

Europe	Europa	[euˈrʊpa]
Asia	Asien	['asiən]
Africa	Afrika	['afrika]
Australia	Australien	[auˈstraliən]

| America | Amerika | [aˈmerika] |
| North America | Nordamerika | ['nʊːɖ aˈmerika] |

South America	Sydamerika	['syd a'merika]
Antarctica	Antarktis	[an'tarktis]
the Arctic	Arktis	['arktis]

76. Cardinal directions

north	norr	['nɔr]
to the north	norrut	['nɔrʉt]
in the north	i norr	[i 'nɔr]
northern (adj)	nordlig	['nʉːdlig]

south	söder (en)	['søːdər]
to the south	söderut	['søːdərʉt]
in the south	i söder	[i 'søːdər]
southern (adj)	syd-, söder	['syd-], ['søːdər]

west	väster (en)	['vɛstər]
to the west	västerut	['vɛstərʉt]
in the west	i väst	[i vɛst]
western (adj)	västra	['vɛstra]

east	öster (en)	['œstər]
to the east	österut	['œstərʉt]
in the east	i öst	[i 'œst]
eastern (adj)	östra	['œstra]

77. Sea. Ocean

sea	hav (ett)	['hav]
ocean	ocean (en)	[ʉsə'an]
gulf (bay)	bukt (en)	['bukt]
straits	sund (ett)	['sund]

land (solid ground)	fastland (ett)	['fast,lʲand]
continent (mainland)	fastland (ett),	['fast,lʲand],
	kontinent (en)	[kɔnti'nɛnt]
island	ö (en)	['øː]
peninsula	halvö (en)	['halʲv,øː]
archipelago	skärgård, arkipelag (en)	['ɧæːr,goːd], [arkipe'lʲag]

bay, cove	bukt (en)	['bukt]
harbor	hamn (en)	['hamn]
lagoon	lagun (en)	[lʲa'gʉːn]
cape	udde (en)	['udə]

atoll	atoll (en)	[a'tɔlʲ]
reef	rev (ett)	['rev]
coral	korall (en)	[kɔ'ralʲ]

coral reef	korallrev (ett)	[kɔ'ralʲˌrev]
deep (adj)	djup	['jɥːp]
depth (deep water)	djup (ett)	['jɥːp]
abyss	avgrund (en)	['avˌgrɵnd]
trench (e.g., Mariana ~)	djuphavsgrav (en)	['jɥːphavsˌgrav]
current (Ocean ~)	ström (en)	['strøːm]
to surround (bathe)	att omge	[at 'ɔmje]
shore	kust (en)	['kust]
coast	kust (en)	['kust]
flow (flood tide)	flod (en)	['flʲud]
ebb (ebb tide)	ebb (en)	['ɛb]
shoal	sandbank (en)	['sandˌbaŋk]
bottom (~ of the sea)	botten (en)	['bɔtən]
wave	våg (en)	['voːg]
crest (~ of a wave)	vågkam (en)	['voːgˌkam]
spume (sea foam)	skum (ett)	['skum]
storm (sea storm)	storm (en)	['stɔrm]
hurricane	orkan (en)	[ɔr'kan]
tsunami	tsunami (en)	[tsu'nami]
calm (dead ~)	stiltje (en)	['stilʲtjə]
quiet, calm (adj)	stilla	['stilʲa]
pole	pol (en)	['pulʲ]
polar (adj)	pol-, polar-	['pulʲ-], [pu'lʲar-]
latitude	latitud (en)	[lʲati'tɥːd]
longitude	longitud (en)	[lʲɔŋi'tɥːd]
parallel	breddgrad (en)	['brɛdˌgrad]
equator	ekvator (en)	[ɛ'kvatur]
sky	himmel (en)	['himəlʲ]
horizon	horisont (en)	[huri'sɔnt]
air	luft (en)	['lɵft]
lighthouse	fyr (en)	['fyr]
to dive (vi)	att dyka	[at 'dyka]
to sink (ab. boat)	att sjunka	[at 'ɧuŋka]
treasures	skatter (pl)	['skatər]

78. Seas' and Oceans' names

Atlantic Ocean	Atlanten	[at'lʲantən]
Indian Ocean	Indiska oceanen	['indiska usə'anən]
Pacific Ocean	Stilla havet	['stilʲa 'havɛt]
Arctic Ocean	Norra ishavet	['nɔra ˌis'havɛt]

Black Sea	Svarta havet	['svaːʈa 'havɛt]
Red Sea	Röda havet	['røːda 'havɛt]
Yellow Sea	Gula havet	['gʉːlʲa 'havɛt]
White Sea	Vita havet	['vita 'havɛt]

Caspian Sea	Kaspiska havet	['kaspiska 'havɛt]
Dead Sea	Döda havet	['døːda 'havɛt]
Mediterranean Sea	Medelhavet	['medəlʲˌhavɛt]

Aegean Sea	Egeiska havet	[ɛ'gejska 'havɛt]
Adriatic Sea	Adriatiska havet	[adri'atiska 'havɛt]

Arabian Sea	Arabiska havet	[a'rabiska 'havɛt]
Sea of Japan	Japanska havet	[ja'panska 'havɛt]
Bering Sea	Beringshavet	['beringsˌhavɛt]
South China Sea	Sydkinesiska havet	['sydɕiˌnesiska 'havɛt]

Coral Sea	Korallhavet	[kɔ'ralʲˌhavɛt]
Tasman Sea	Tasmanhavet	[tas'manˌhavɛt]
Caribbean Sea	Karibiska havet	[ka'ribiska 'havɛt]

Barents Sea	Barentshavet	['barɛntsˌhavɛt]
Kara Sea	Karahavet	['karaˌhavɛt]

North Sea	Nordsjön	['nʊːɖˌɧøːn]
Baltic Sea	Östersjön	['œstɛːˌɧøːn]
Norwegian Sea	Norska havet	['nɔːʂka 'havɛt]

79. Mountains

mountain	berg (ett)	['bɛrj]
mountain range	bergskedja (en)	['bɛrjˌɕedja]
mountain ridge	bergsrygg (en)	['bɛrjsˌrʏg]

summit, top	topp (en)	['tɔp]
peak	tinne (en)	['tinə]
foot (~ of the mountain)	fot (en)	['fʊt]
slope (mountainside)	sluttning (en)	['slʉːtniŋ]

volcano	vulkan (en)	[vulʲ'kan]
active volcano	verksam vulkan (en)	['vɛrksam vulʲ'kan]
dormant volcano	slocknad vulkan (en)	['slʲoknad vulʲ'kan]

eruption	utbrott (ett)	['ʉtˌbrɔt]
crater	krater (en)	['kratər]
magma	magma (en)	['magma]
lava	lava (en)	['lʲava]
molten (~ lava)	glödgad	['glʲœdgad]
canyon	kanjon (en)	['kanjon]
gorge	klyfta (en)	['klʲyfta]

| crevice | skreva (en) | ['skreva] |
| abyss (chasm) | avgrund (en) | ['av‚grɵnd] |

pass, col	pass (ett)	['pas]
plateau	platå (en)	[plʲa'to:]
cliff	klippa (en)	['klipa]
hill	kulle, backe (en)	['kulʲə], ['bakə]

glacier	glaciär, jökel (en)	[glʲas'jæ:r], ['jø:kəlʲ]
waterfall	vattenfall (ett)	['vatən‚falʲ]
geyser	gejser (en)	['gɛjsər]
lake	sjö (en)	['ŋø:]

plain	slätt (en)	['slʲæt]
landscape	landskap (ett)	['lʲaŋ‚skap]
echo	eko (ett)	['ɛkʊ]

alpinist	alpinist (en)	['alʲpi‚nist]
rock climber	bergsbestigare (en)	['bɛrjs‚be'stigarə]
to conquer (in climbing)	att erövra	[at ɛ'rœvra]
climb (an easy ~)	bestigning (en)	[be'stigniŋ]

80. Mountains names

The Alps	Alperna	['alʲpɛ:ŋa]
Mont Blanc	Mont Blanc	[‚mɔn'blʲaŋ]
The Pyrenees	Pyrenéerna	[pyre'neæ:ŋa]

The Carpathians	Karpaterna	[kar'patɛ:ŋa]
The Ural Mountains	Uralbergen	[ɵ'ralʲ‚bɛrjən]
The Caucasus Mountains	Kaukasus	['kaukasus]
Mount Elbrus	Elbrus	['ɛlʲbrɵs]

The Altai Mountains	Altaj	[alʲ'taj]
The Tian Shan	Tian Shan	[ti'an ʃan]
The Pamir Mountains	Pamir	[pa'mir]
The Himalayas	Himalaya	[hi'malʲaja]
Mount Everest	Everest	[ɛve'rɛst]

| The Andes | Anderna | ['andɛ:ŋa] |
| Mount Kilimanjaro | Kilimanjaro | [kiliman'jarɵ] |

81. Rivers

river	älv, flod (en)	['ɛlʲv], ['flʲʊd]
spring (natural source)	källa (en)	['ɕɛlʲa]
riverbed (river channel)	flodbädd (en)	['flʲʊd‚bɛd]
basin (river valley)	flodbassäng (en)	['flʲʊd‚ba'sɛŋ]

to flow into ...	att mynna ut ...	[at 'mʏna ʉt ...]
tributary	biflod (en)	['biˌflʉd]
bank (of river)	strand (en)	['strand]

current (stream)	ström (en)	['strøːm]
downstream (adv)	nedströms	['nɛdˌstrœms]
upstream (adv)	motströms	['mʉtˌstrœms]

inundation	översvämning (en)	['øːvəˌsvɛmniŋ]
flooding	flöde (ett)	['flʲøːdə]
to overflow (vi)	att flöda över	[at 'flʲøːda ˌøːvər]
to flood (vt)	att översvämma	[at 'øːvəˌsvɛma]

| shallow (shoal) | grund (ett) | ['grʉnd] |
| rapids | forsar (pl) | [fo'ʂar] |

dam	damm (en)	['dam]
canal	kanal (en)	[ka'nalʲ]
reservoir (artificial lake)	reservoar (ett)	[resɛrvʊ'aːr]
sluice, lock	sluss (en)	['slʉːs]

water body (pond, etc.)	vattensamling (en)	['vatənˌsamliŋ]
swamp (marshland)	myr, mosse (en)	['myr], ['mʊsə]
bog, marsh	gungfly (ett)	['guŋˌfly]
whirlpool	strömvirvel (en)	['strøːmˌvirvəlʲ]

stream (brook)	bäck (en)	['bɛk]
drinking (ab. water)	dricks-	['driks-]
fresh (~ water)	söt-, färsk-	['søːt-], ['fæːʂk-]

ice	is (en)	['is]
to freeze over	att frysa till	[at 'frysa tilʲ]
(ab. river, etc.)		

82. Rivers' names

| Seine | Seine | ['sɛːn] |
| Loire | Loire | [lʲʊ'aːr] |

Thames	Themsen	['tɛmsən]
Rhine	Rhen	['ren]
Danube	Donau	['dɔnaʊ]

Volga	Volga	['vɔlʲga]
Don	Don	['dɔn]
Lena	Lena	['lʲena]

Yellow River	Hwang-ho	[huaŋ'hʊ]
Yangtze	Yangtze	['jɑŋtsə]
Mekong	Mekong	[me'kɔŋ]

Ganges	Ganges	['gaŋəs]
Nile River	Nilen	['nilʲen]
Congo River	Kongo	['kɔngʊ]
Okavango River	Okavango	[ɔka'vangʊ]
Zambezi River	Zambezi	[sam'besi]
Limpopo River	Limpopo	[lim'pɔpɔ]
Mississippi River	Mississippi	[misi'sipi]

83. Forest

| forest, wood | skog (en) | ['skʊg] |
| forest (as adj) | skogs- | ['skʊgs-] |

thick forest	tät skog (en)	['tɛt ˌskʊg]
grove	lund (en)	['lʉnd]
forest clearing	glänta (en)	['glʲɛnta]

| thicket | snår (ett) | ['snoːr] |
| scrubland | buskterräng (en) | ['busk tɛ'rɛŋ] |

| footpath (troddenpath) | stig (en) | ['stig] |
| gully | ravin (en) | [ra'vin] |

tree	träd (ett)	['trɛːd]
leaf	löv (ett)	['lʲøːv]
leaves (foliage)	löv, lövverk (ett)	['lʲøːv], ['lʲøːværk]

fall of leaves	lövfällning (en)	['lʲøːvˌfɛlʲniŋ]
to fall (ab. leaves)	att falla	[at 'falʲa]
top (of the tree)	trädtopp (en)	['trɛːˌtɔp]

branch	gren, kvist (en)	['gren], ['kvist]
bough	gren (en)	['gren]
bud (on shrub, tree)	knopp (en)	['knɔp]
needle (of pine tree)	nål (en)	['noːlʲ]
pine cone	kotte (en)	['kɔtə]

hollow (in a tree)	trädhål (ett)	['trɛːdˌhoːlʲ]
nest	bo (ett)	['bʊ]
burrow (animal hole)	lya, håla (en)	['lʲya], ['hoːlʲa]

trunk	stam (en)	['stam]
root	rot (en)	['rʊt]
bark	bark (en)	['bark]
moss	mossa (en)	['mɔsa]

to uproot (remove trees or tree stumps)	att rycka upp med rötterna	[at 'rʏka up me 'rœttɛːŋa]
to chop down	att fälla	[at 'fɛlʲa]
to deforest (vt)	att hugga ner	[at 'huga ner]

tree stump	stubbe (en)	['stubə]
campfire	bål (ett)	['bo:lʲ]
forest fire	skogsbrand (en)	['skʊgs͵brand]
to extinguish (vt)	att släcka	[at 'slʲɛka]

forest ranger	skogsvakt (en)	['skʊgs͵vakt]
protection	värn, skydd (ett)	['væ:n], [ɧyd]
to protect (~ nature)	att skydda	[at 'ɧyda]
poacher	tjuvskytt (en)	['ɕɵ:v͵ɧyt]
steel trap	sax (en)	['saks]

| to gather, to pick (vt) | att plocka | [at 'plʲɔka] |
| to lose one's way | att gå vilse | [at 'go: 'vilʲsə] |

84. Natural resources

natural resources	naturresurser (pl)	[na'tɵ:r re'surʂər]
minerals	mineraler (pl)	[mine'ralʲər]
deposits	fyndigheter (pl)	['fʏndi͵hetər]
field (e.g., oilfield)	fält (ett)	['fɛlʲt]

to mine (extract)	att utvinna	[at 'ɵt͵vina]
mining (extraction)	utvinning (en)	['ɵt͵viniŋ]
ore	malm (en)	['malʲm]
mine (e.g., for coal)	gruva (en)	['grɵva]
shaft (mine ~)	gruvschakt (ett)	['grɵ:v͵ɧakt]
miner	gruvarbetare (en)	['grɵ:v͵ar'betarə]

| gas (natural ~) | gas (en) | ['gas] |
| gas pipeline | gasledning (en) | ['gas͵lʲedniŋ] |

oil (petroleum)	olja (en)	['ɔlja]
oil pipeline	oljeledning (en)	['ɔlje͵lʲedniŋ]
oil well	oljekälla (en)	['ɔlje͵ɕæla]
derrick (tower)	borrtorn (ett)	['bɔr͵tʊ:n]
tanker	tankfartyg (ett)	['taŋk͵fa:'tyg]

sand	sand (en)	['sand]
limestone	kalksten (en)	[kalʲk͵sten]
gravel	grus (ett)	['grɵ:s]
peat	torv (en)	['tɔrv]
clay	lera (en)	['lʲera]
coal	kol (ett)	['kɔlʲ]

iron (ore)	järn (ett)	['jæ:ɳ]
gold	guld (ett)	['gulʲd]
silver	silver (ett)	['silʲvər]
nickel	nickel (en)	['nikəlʲ]
copper	koppar (en)	['kopar]
zinc	zink (en)	['siŋk]

manganese	mangan (en)	[man'gan]
mercury	kvicksilver (ett)	['kvik‚sil'vər]
lead	bly (ett)	['bli'y]

mineral	mineral (ett)	[minə'ral']
crystal	kristall (en)	[kri'stal']
marble	marmor (en)	['marmʊr]
uranium	uran (ett)	[ʉ'ran]

85. Weather

weather	väder (ett)	['vɛ:dər]
weather forecast	väderprognos (en)	['vɛ:dər‚prɔg'nɔ:s]
temperature	temperatur (en)	[tɛmpəra'tʉ:r]
thermometer	termometer (en)	[tɛrmʊ'metər]
barometer	barometer (en)	[barʊ'metər]

humid (adj)	fuktig	['fu:ktig]
humidity	fuktighet (en)	['fu:ktig‚het]
heat (extreme ~)	hetta (en)	['hɛta]
hot (torrid)	het	['het]
it's hot	det är hett	[dɛ æ:r 'hɛt]

it's warm	det är varmt	[dɛ æ:r varmt]
warm (moderately hot)	varm	['varm]

it's cold	det är kallt	[dɛ æ:r 'kal't]
cold (adj)	kall	['kal']

sun	sol (en)	['sʊl']
to shine (vi)	att skina	[at 'ɧina]
sunny (day)	solig	['sʊlig]
to come up (vi)	att gå upp	[at 'go: 'up]
to set (vi)	att gå ner	[at 'go: ‚ner]

cloud	moln (ett), sky (en)	['mɔl'n], ['ɧy]
cloudy (adj)	molnig	['mɔl'nig]
rain cloud	regnmoln (ett)	['rɛgn‚mɔl'n]
somber (gloomy)	mörk, mulen	['mœ:rk], ['mʉ:l'en]

rain	regn (ett)	['rɛgn]
it's raining	det regnar	[dɛ 'rɛgnar]
rainy (~ day, weather)	regnväders-	['rɛgn‚vɛdəʂ-]
to drizzle (vi)	att duggregna	[at 'dug‚rɛgna]

pouring rain	hällande regn (ett)	['hɛl'andə 'rɛgn]
downpour	spöregn (ett)	['spø:‚rɛgn]
heavy (e.g., ~ rain)	kraftigt, häftigt	['kraftigt], ['hɛftigt]
puddle	pöl, vattenpuss (en)	['pø:l'], ['vatən‚pus]
to get wet (in rain)	att bli våt	[at bli 'vo:t]

fog (mist)	dimma (en)	['dima]
foggy	dimmig	['dimig]
snow	snö (en)	['snø:]
it's snowing	det snöar	[dɛ 'snø:ar]

86. Severe weather. Natural disasters

thunderstorm	åskväder (ett)	['ɔsk‚vɛdər]
lightning (~ strike)	blixt (en)	['blikst]
to flash (vi)	att blixtra	[at 'blikstra]

thunder	åska (en)	['ɔska]
to thunder (vi)	att åska	[at 'ɔska]
it's thundering	det åskar	[dɛ 'ɔskar]

| hail | hagel (ett) | ['hagəlⁱ] |
| it's hailing | det haglar | [dɛ 'haglⁱar] |

| to flood (vt) | att översvämma | [at 'ø:və‚svɛma] |
| flood, inundation | översvämning (en) | ['ø:və‚svɛmniŋ] |

earthquake	jordskalv (ett)	['jʊːd‚skalv]
tremor, quake	skalv (ett)	['skalⁱv]
epicenter	epicentrum (ett)	[ɛpi'sɛntrum]

| eruption | utbrott (ett) | ['ʉt‚brɔt] |
| lava | lava (en) | ['lⁱava] |

twister	tromb (en)	['trɔmb]
tornado	tornado (en)	[tʊ'ŋadʊ]
typhoon	tyfon (en)	[ty'fɔn]

hurricane	orkan (en)	[ɔr'kan]
storm	storm (en)	['stɔrm]
tsunami	tsunami (en)	[tsu'nami]

cyclone	cyklon (en)	[tsʏ'klⁱɔn]
bad weather	oväder (ett)	[ʊ'vɛːdər]
fire (accident)	brand (en)	['brand]
disaster	katastrof (en)	[kata'strɔf]
meteorite	meteorit (en)	[meteʊ'rit]

avalanche	lavin (en)	[lⁱa'vin]
snowslide	snöskred, snöras (ett)	['snø:‚skred], ['snø:‚ras]
blizzard	snöstorm (en)	['snø:‚stɔrm]
snowstorm	snöstorm (en)	['snø:‚stɔrm]

FAUNA

87. Mammals. Predators

predator	rovdjur (ett)	['rʊvˌjɐːr]
tiger	tiger (en)	['tigər]
lion	lejon (ett)	['lʲejɔn]
wolf	ulv (en)	['ulʲv]
fox	räv (en)	['rɛːv]

jaguar	jaguar (en)	[jaguar]
leopard	leopard (en)	[lʲeʊ'paːd]
cheetah	gepard (en)	[je'paːd]

black panther	panter (en)	['pantər]
puma	puma (en)	['pɐːma]
snow leopard	snöleopard (en)	['snøː lʲeʊ'paːd]
lynx	lodjur (ett), lo (en)	['lʲʊjɐːr], ['lʲʊ]

coyote	koyot, prärievarg (en)	[kɔ'jʊt], ['præːrieˌvarj]
jackal	sjakal (en)	[ʂa'kalʲ]
hyena	hyena (en)	[hy'ena]

88. Wild animals

| animal | djur (ett) | ['jɐːr] |
| beast (animal) | best (en), djur (ett) | ['bɛst], ['jɐːr] |

squirrel	ekorre (en)	['ɛkɔrə]
hedgehog	igelkott (en)	['igəlʲˌkɔt]
hare	hare (en)	['harə]
rabbit	kanin (en)	[ka'nin]

badger	grävling (en)	['grɛvliŋ]
raccoon	tvättbjörn (en)	['tvætˌbjøːɳ]
hamster	hamster (en)	['hamstər]
marmot	murmeldjur (ett)	['murməlʲjɐːr]

mole	mullvad (en)	['mulʲˌvad]
mouse	mus (en)	['mɐːs]
rat	råtta (en)	['rɔta]
bat	fladdermus (en)	['flʲadərˌmɐːs]
ermine	hermelin (en)	[hɛrme'lin]
sable	sobel (en)	['sɔbəlʲ]

marten	mård (en)	['moːɖ]
weasel	vessla (en)	['vɛslʲa]
mink	mink (en)	['miŋk]

| beaver | bäver (en) | ['bɛːvər] |
| otter | utter (en) | ['ʉːtər] |

horse	häst (en)	['hɛst]
moose	älg (en)	['ɛlj]
deer	hjort (en)	['jʉːt]
camel	kamel (en)	[ka'melʲ]

bison	bison (en)	['bisɔn]
aurochs	uroxe (en)	['ʉˌrɔksə]
buffalo	buffel (en)	['bufəlʲ]

zebra	sebra (en)	['sebra]
antelope	antilop (en)	[anti'lʲʊp]
roe deer	rådjur (ett)	['rɔːjɵːr]
fallow deer	dovhjort (en)	['dɔvˌjʉːt]
chamois	gems (en)	['jɛms]
wild boar	vildsvin (ett)	['vilʲdˌsvin]

whale	val (en)	['valʲ]
seal	säl (en)	['sɛːlʲ]
walrus	valross (en)	['valʲˌrɔs]
fur seal	pälssäl (en)	['pɛlʲsˌsɛlʲ]
dolphin	delfin (en)	[dɛlʲ'fin]

bear	björn (en)	['bjøːɳ]
polar bear	isbjörn (en)	['isˌbjøːɳ]
panda	panda (en)	['panda]

monkey	apa (en)	['apa]
chimpanzee	schimpans (en)	[ɧim'pans]
orangutan	orangutang (en)	[ʊ'raŋɵˌtaŋ]
gorilla	gorilla (en)	[gɔ'rilʲa]
macaque	makak (en)	[ma'kak]
gibbon	gibbon (en)	[gi'bʊn]

elephant	elefant (en)	[ɛlʲe'fant]
rhinoceros	noshörning (en)	['nʊsˌhøːɳiŋ]
giraffe	giraff (en)	[ɧi'raf]
hippopotamus	flodhäst (en)	['flʲʊdˌhɛst]

| kangaroo | känguru (en) | ['ɕɛŋgurʊ] |
| koala (bear) | koala (en) | [kʊ'alʲa] |

mongoose	mangust, mungo (en)	['mangust], ['muŋgʊ]
chinchilla	chinchilla (en)	[ʃin'ʃilʲa]
skunk	skunk (en)	['skuŋk]
porcupine	piggsvin (ett)	['pigˌsvin]

89. Domestic animals

cat	katt (en)	['kat]
tomcat	hankatt (en)	['han‚kat]
dog	hund (en)	['hund]
horse	häst (en)	['hɛst]
stallion (male horse)	hingst (en)	['hiŋst]
mare	sto (ett)	['stʊ:]
cow	ko (en)	['kɔ:]
bull	tjur (en)	['ɕʉ:r]
ox	oxe (en)	['ʊksə]
sheep (ewe)	får (ett)	['fo:r]
ram	bagge (en)	['bagə]
goat	get (en)	['jet]
billy goat, he-goat	getabock (en)	['jeta‚bɔk]
donkey	åsna (en)	['ɔsna]
mule	mula (en)	['mʉlʲa]
pig, hog	svin (ett)	['svin]
piglet	griskulting (en)	['gris‚kulʲtiŋ]
rabbit	kanin (en)	[ka'nin]
hen (chicken)	höna (en)	['hø:na]
rooster	tupp (en)	['tup]
duck	anka (en)	['aŋka]
drake	andrik, andrake (en)	['andrik], ['andrakə]
goose	gås (en)	['go:s]
tom turkey, gobbler	kalkontupp (en)	[kalʲ'kʊn‚tup]
turkey (hen)	kalkonhöna (en)	[kalʲ'kʊn‚hø:na]
domestic animals	husdjur (pl)	['hʉs‚jʉ:r]
tame (e.g., ~ hamster)	tam	['tam]
to tame (vt)	att tämja	[at 'tɛmja]
to breed (vt)	att avla, att föda upp	[at 'avlʲa], [at 'fø:da up]
farm	farm, lantgård (en)	[farm], ['lʲant‚go:d]
poultry	fjäderfä (ett)	['fjɛ:dər‚fɛ:]
cattle	boskap (en)	['bʊskap]
herd (cattle)	hjord (en)	['jʊ:d]
stable	stall (ett)	['stalʲ]
pigpen	svinstia (en)	['svin‚stia]
cowshed	ladugård (en), kostall (ett)	['lʲadʉ‚go:d], ['kostalʲ]
rabbit hutch	kaninbur (en)	[ka'nin‚bʉ:r]
hen house	hönshus (ett)	['hø:ns‚hʉs]

90. Birds

bird	fågel (en)	['foːgəlʲ]
pigeon	duva (en)	['dʉːva]
sparrow	sparv (en)	['sparv]
tit (great tit)	talgoxe (en)	['taljʊksə]
magpie	skata (en)	['skata]

raven	korp (en)	['kɔrp]
crow	kråka (en)	['kroːka]
jackdaw	kaja (en)	['kaja]
rook	råka (en)	['roːka]

duck	anka (en)	['aŋka]
goose	gås (en)	['goːs]
pheasant	fasan (en)	[fa'san]

eagle	örn (en)	['øːɳ]
hawk	hök (en)	['høːk]
falcon	falk (en)	['falʲk]
vulture	gam (en)	['gam]
condor (Andean ~)	kondor (en)	['kɔnˌdor]

swan	svan (en)	['svan]
crane	trana (en)	['trana]
stork	stork (en)	['stɔrk]

parrot	papegoja (en)	[pape'gɔja]
hummingbird	kolibri (en)	['kɔlibri]
peacock	påfågel (en)	['poːˌfoːgəlʲ]

ostrich	struts (en)	['struts]
heron	häger (en)	['hɛːgər]
flamingo	flamingo (en)	[flʲa'mingɔ]
pelican	pelikan (en)	[peli'kan]

| nightingale | näktergal (en) | ['nɛktəˌgalʲ] |
| swallow | svala (en) | ['svalʲa] |

thrush	trast (en)	['trast]
song thrush	sångtrast (en)	['sɔŋˌtrast]
blackbird	koltrast (en)	['kɔlʲˌtrast]

swift	tornseglare, tornsvala (en)	['tʊːɳˌseglarə], ['tʊːɳˌsvalʲa]
lark	lärka (en)	['lʲæːrka]
quail	vaktel (en)	['vaktəlʲ]

woodpecker	hackspett (en)	['hakˌspet]
cuckoo	gök (en)	['jøːk]
owl	uggla (en)	['uglʲa]

eagle owl	berguv (en)	['bɛrj,ʉːv]
wood grouse	tjäder (en)	['ɕɛːdər]
black grouse	orre (en)	['ɔrə]
partridge	rapphöna (en)	['rap,høːna]

starling	stare (en)	['starə]
canary	kanariefågel (en)	[ka'nariə,foːgəlʲ]
hazel grouse	järpe (en)	['jæːrpə]
chaffinch	bofink (en)	['bʊ,fiŋk]
bullfinch	domherre (en)	['dʊmhɛrə]

seagull	mås (en)	['moːs]
albatross	albatross (en)	['alʲba,trɔs]
penguin	pingvin (en)	[piŋ'vin]

91. Fish. Marine animals

bream	brax (en)	['braks]
carp	karp (en)	['karp]
perch	ábborre (en)	['abɔrə]
catfish	mal (en)	['malʲ]
pike	gädda (en)	['jɛda]

salmon	lax (en)	['lʲaks]
sturgeon	stör (en)	['støːr]

herring	sill (en)	['silʲ]
Atlantic salmon	atlanterhavslax (en)	[at'lantərhav,lʲaks]
mackerel	makrill (en)	['makrilʲ]
flatfish	rödspätta (en)	['røːd,spæta]

zander, pike perch	gös (en)	['jøːs]
cod	torsk (en)	['tɔːʂk]
tuna	tonfisk (en)	['tʊn,fisk]
trout	öring (en)	['øːriŋ]

eel	ål (en)	['oːlʲ]
electric ray	elektrisk rocka (en)	[ɛ'lʲektrisk,rɔka]
moray eel	muräna (en)	[mʉ'rɛna]
piranha	piraya (en)	[pi'raja]

shark	haj (en)	['haj]
dolphin	delfin (en)	[dɛlʲ'fin]
whale	val (en)	['valʲ]

crab	krabba (en)	['kraba]
jellyfish	manet, medusa (en)	[ma'net], [me'dʉsa]
octopus	bläckfisk (en)	['blʲɛk,fisk]
starfish	sjöstjärna (en)	['ɧøː,ɧæːŋa]
sea urchin	sjöpiggsvin (ett)	['ɧøː,pigsvin]

seahorse	sjöhäst (en)	['ŋø:ˌhɛst]
oyster	ostron (ett)	['ʊstrʊn]
shrimp	räka (en)	['rɛ:ka]
lobster	hummer (en)	['humər]
spiny lobster	languster (en)	[lʲaŋ'gustər]

92. Amphibians. Reptiles

| snake | orm (en) | ['ʊrm] |
| venomous (snake) | giftig | ['jiftig] |

viper	huggorm (en)	['hʉgˌʊrm]
cobra	kobra (en)	['kɔbra]
python	pytonorm (en)	[py'tɔnˌʊrm]
boa	boaorm (en)	['bʊaˌʊrm]

grass snake	snok (en)	['snʊk]
rattle snake	skallerorm (en)	['skalʲerˌʊrm]
anaconda	anaconda (en)	[ana'kɔnda]

lizard	ödla (en)	['ødlʲa]
iguana	iguana (en)	[igu'ana]
monitor lizard	varan (en)	[va'ran]
salamander	salamander (en)	[salʲa'mandər]
chameleon	kameleont (en)	[kamelʲe'ɔnt]
scorpion	skorpion (en)	[skɔrpi'ʊn]

turtle	sköldpadda (en)	['ŋœlʲdˌpada]
frog	groda (en)	['grʊda]
toad	padda (en)	['pada]
crocodile	krokodil (en)	[krɔkɔ'dilʲ]

93. Insects

insect, bug	insekt (en)	['insɛkt]
butterfly	fjäril (en)	['fʲæ:rilʲ]
ant	myra (en)	['myra]
fly	fluga (en)	['flʉ:ga]
mosquito	mygga (en)	['mɤga]
beetle	skalbagge (en)	['skalʲˌbagə]

wasp	geting (en)	['jɛtiŋ]
bee	bi (ett)	['bi]
bumblebee	humla (en)	['humlʲa]
gadfly (botfly)	styngfluga (en)	['stɤŋˌflʉ:ga]

| spider | spindel (en) | ['spindəlʲ] |
| spiderweb | spindelnät (ett) | ['spindəlˌnɛ:t] |

dragonfly	trollslända (en)	['trɔlʲˌslʲɛnda]
grasshopper	gräshoppa (en)	['grɛsˌhɔpa]
moth (night butterfly)	nattfjäril (en)	['natˌfjæːrilʲ]

cockroach	kackerlacka (en)	['kakɛːˌlʲaka]
tick	fästing (en)	['fɛstiŋ]
flea	loppa (en)	['lʲɔpa]
midge	knott (ett)	['knot]

locust	vandringsgräs-hoppa (en)	['vandriŋˌgrɛs 'hɔparə]
snail	snigel (en)	['snigəlʲ]
cricket	syrsa (en)	['syʂa]
lightning bug	lysmask (en)	['lʲysˌmask]
ladybug	nyckelpiga (en)	['nʏkəlʲˌpiga]
cockchafer	ollonborre (en)	['ɔlʲɔnˌbɔrə]

leech	igel (en)	['iːgəlʲ]
caterpillar	fjärilslarv (en)	['fjæːrilʲsˌlʲarv]
earthworm	daggmask (en)	['dagˌmask]
larva	larv (en)	['lʲarv]

FLORA

94. Trees

tree	träd (ett)	['trɛ:d]
deciduous (adj)	löv-	['lø:v-]
coniferous (adj)	barr-	['bar-]
evergreen (adj)	eviggrönt	['ɛviˌɡrœnt]

apple tree	äppelträd (ett)	['ɛpelˌtrɛd]
pear tree	päronträd (ett)	['pæ:rɔnˌtrɛd]
sweet cherry tree	fågelbärsträd (ett)	['fo:ɡəlˌbæ:ʂˌtrɛd]
sour cherry tree	körsbärsträd (ett)	['ɕø:ʂbæ:ʂˌtrɛd]
plum tree	plommonträd (ett)	['plʲʊmɔnˌtrɛd]

birch	björk (en)	['bjœrk]
oak	ek (en)	['ɛk]
linden tree	lind (en)	['lind]
aspen	asp (en)	['asp]
maple	lönn (en)	['lʲøn]

spruce	gran (en)	['ɡran]
pine	tall (en)	['talʲ]
larch	lärk (en)	['lʲæ:rk]
fir tree	silvergran (en)	['silʲvərˌɡran]
cedar	ceder (en)	['sedər]

poplar	poppel (en)	['pɔpəlʲ]
rowan	rönn (en)	['rœn]
willow	pil (en)	['pilʲ]
alder	al (en)	['alʲ]

| beech | bok (en) | ['bʊk] |
| elm | alm (en) | ['alʲm] |

| ash (tree) | ask (en) | ['ask] |
| chestnut | kastanjeträd (ett) | [ka'stanjəˌtrɛd] |

magnolia	magnolia (en)	[maŋ'nʊlia]
palm tree	palm (en)	['palʲm]
cypress	cypress (en)	[sʏ'prɛs]

mangrove	mangroveträd (ett)	[maŋ'rɔvəˌtrɛd]
baobab	apbrödsträd (ett)	['apbrødsˌtrɛd]
eucalyptus	eukalyptus (en)	[euka'lʲyptʉs]
sequoia	sequoia (en)	[sek'vɔja]

95. Shrubs

bush	buske (en)	['buskə]
shrub	buske (en)	['buskə]
grapevine	vinranka (en)	['vin‚raŋka]
vineyard	vingård (en)	['vin‚go:d]
raspberry bush	hallonsnår (ett)	['halʲon‚sno:r]
blackcurrant bush	svarta vinbär (ett)	['sva:ʈa 'vinbæ:r]
redcurrant bush	röd vinbärsbuske (en)	['rø:d 'vinbæ:ʂ‚buskə]
gooseberry bush	krusbärsbuske (en)	['krʉ:sbæ:ʂ‚buskə]
acacia	akacia (en)	[a'kasia]
barberry	berberis (en)	['bɛrberis]
jasmine	jasmin (en)	[has'min]
juniper	en (en)	['en]
rosebush	rosenbuske (en)	['rʊsən‚buskə]
dog rose	stenros, hundros (en)	['stenrʊs], ['hundrʊs]

96. Fruits. Berries

fruit	frukt (en)	['frʉkt]
fruits	frukter (pl)	['frʉktər]
apple	äpple (ett)	['ɛplʲe]
pear	päron (ett)	['pæ:rɔn]
plum	plommon (ett)	['plʲʊmɔn]
strawberry (garden ~)	jordgubbe (en)	['jʊ:d‚gubə]
sour cherry	körsbär (ett)	['ɕø:ʂ‚bæ:r]
sweet cherry	fågelbär (ett)	['fo:gəlʲ‚bæ:r]
grape	druva (en)	['drʉ:va]
raspberry	hallon (ett)	['halʲon]
blackcurrant	svarta vinbär (ett)	['sva:ʈa 'vinbæ:r]
redcurrant	röda vinbär (ett)	['rø:da 'vinbæ:r]
gooseberry	krusbär (ett)	['krʉ:s‚bæ:r]
cranberry	tranbär (ett)	['tran‚bæ:r]
orange	apelsin (en)	[apɛlʲ'sin]
mandarin	mandarin (en)	[manda'rin]
pineapple	ananas (en)	['ananas]
banana	banan (en)	['banan]
date	dadel (en)	['dadəlʲ]
lemon	citron (en)	[si'trʊn]
apricot	aprikos (en)	[apri'kʊs]
peach	persika (en)	['pɛʂika]

| kiwi | kiwi (en) | ['kivi] |
| grapefruit | grapefrukt (en) | ['grɛjp‚frʉkt] |

berry	bär (ett)	['bæ:r]
berries	bär (pl)	['bæ:r]
cowberry	lingon (ett)	['liŋɔn]
wild strawberry	skogssmultron (ett)	['skʊgs‚smulˈtrɔ:n]
bilberry	blåbär (ett)	['blʲo:‚bæ:r]

97. Flowers. Plants

| flower | blomma (en) | ['blʲʊma] |
| bouquet (of flowers) | bukett (en) | [bʉ'kɛt] |

rose (flower)	ros (en)	['rʊs]
tulip	tulpan (en)	[tulʲ'pan]
carnation	nejlika (en)	['nɛjlika]
gladiolus	gladiolus (en)	[glʲadi'olʉ:s]

cornflower	blåklint (en)	['blʲo:‚klint]
harebell	blåklocka (en)	['blʲo:‚klʲɔka]
dandelion	maskros (en)	['maskrʊs]
camomile	kamomill (en)	[kamɔ'milʲ]

aloe	aloe (en)	['alʲʊe]
cactus	kaktus (en)	['kaktus]
rubber plant, ficus	fikus (en)	['fikus]

lily	lilja (en)	['lilja]
geranium	geranium (en)	[je'ranium]
hyacinth	hyacint (en)	[hya'sint]

mimosa	mimosa (en)	[mi'mɔ:sa]
narcissus	narciss (en)	[nar'sis]
nasturtium	blomsterkrasse (en)	['blʲomstər‚krasə]

orchid	orkidé (en)	[ɔrki'de:]
peony	pion (en)	[pi'ʊn]
violet	viol (en)	[vi'ʊlʲ]

pansy	styvmorsviol (en)	['styvmʊrs vi'ʊlʲ]
forget-me-not	förgätmigej (en)	[fø‚rʲæt mi 'gej]
daisy	tusensköna (en)	['tʉ:sən‚ɧø:na]

poppy	vallmo (en)	['valʲmʊ]
hemp	hampa (en)	['hampa]
mint	mynta (en)	['mʏnta]

| lily of the valley | liljekonvalje (en) | ['lilje kʊn 'valjə] |
| snowdrop | snödropp (en) | ['snø:‚drop] |

nettle	nässla (en)	['nɛslʲa]
sorrel	syra (en)	['syra]
water lily	näckros (en)	['nɛkrʊs]
fern	ormbunke (en)	['ʊrmˌbʊŋkə]
lichen	lav (en)	['lʲav]
greenhouse (tropical ~)	drivhus (ett)	['drivˌhʉs]
lawn	gräsplan, gräsmatta (en)	['grɛsˌplan], ['grɛsˌmata]
flowerbed	blomsterrabatt (en)	['blʲomstərˌrabat]
plant	växt (en)	['vɛkst]
grass	gräs (ett)	['grɛːs]
blade of grass	grässtrå (ett)	['grɛːsˌstroː]
leaf	löv (ett)	['lʲøːv]
petal	kronblad (ett)	['krɔnˌblʲad]
stem	stjälk (en)	['ɧɛlʲk]
tuber	rotknöl (en)	['rʊtˌknøːlʲ]
young plant (shoot)	ung planta (en)	['uŋ 'planta]
thorn	törne (ett)	['tøːɳə]
to blossom (vi)	att blomma	[at 'blʲʊma]
to fade, to wither	att vissna	[at 'visna]
smell (odor)	lukt (en)	['lʉkt]
to cut (flowers)	att skära av	[at 'ɧæːra av]
to pick (a flower)	att plocka	[at 'plʲɔka]

98. Cereals, grains

grain	korn, spannmål (ett)	['kʊːɳ], ['spanˌmoːlʲ]
cereal crops	spannmål (ett)	['spanˌmoːlʲ]
ear (of barley, etc.)	ax (ett)	['aks]
wheat	vete (ett)	['vetə]
rye	råg (en)	['roːg]
oats	havre (en)	['havrə]
millet	hirs (en)	['hyʂ]
barley	korn (ett)	['kʊːɳ]
corn	majs (en)	['majs]
rice	ris (ett)	['ris]
buckwheat	bovete (ett)	['bʊˌvetə]
pea plant	ärt (en)	['æːʈ]
kidney bean	böna (en)	['bøna]
soy	soja (en)	['sɔja]
lentil	lins (en)	['lins]
beans (pulse crops)	bönor (pl)	['bønʊr]

COUNTRIES OF THE WORLD

99. Countries. Part 1

Afghanistan	**Afghanistan**	[af'gani‚stan]
Albania	**Albanien**	[alʲ'baniǝn]
Argentina	**Argentina**	[argɛn'tina]
Armenia	**Armenien**	[ar'meniǝn]
Australia	**Australien**	[au'straliǝn]
Austria	**Österrike**	['œstɛ‚rikǝ]
Azerbaijan	**Azerbajdzjan**	[asɛrbaj'dʒʲan]
The Bahamas	**Bahamas**	[ba'hamas]
Bangladesh	**Bangladesh**	[banglʲa'dɛʃ]
Belarus	**Vitryssland**	['vit‚rʏslʲand]
Belgium	**Belgien**	['bɛlʲgiǝn]
Bolivia	**Bolivia**	[bʊ'livia]
Bosnia and Herzegovina	**Bosnien-Hercegovina**	['bɔsniǝn hɛrsǝgɔ'vina]
Brazil	**Brasilien**	[bra'siliǝn]
Bulgaria	**Bulgarien**	[bʉlʲ'gariǝn]
Cambodia	**Kambodja**	[kam'bɔdja]
Canada	**Kanada**	['kanada]
Chile	**Chile**	['ɕiːlʲe]
China	**Kina**	['ɕina]
Colombia	**Colombia**	[kɔ'lʲʊmbia]
Croatia	**Kroatien**	[krʊ'atiǝn]
Cuba	**Kuba**	['kʉːba]
Cyprus	**Cypern**	['sypɛːŋ]
Czech Republic	**Tjeckien**	['ɕɛkiǝn]
Denmark	**Danmark**	['daŋmark]
Dominican Republic	**Dominikanska republiken**	[domini'kanska repu'blikǝn]
Ecuador	**Ecuador**	[ɛkva'dʊr]
Egypt	**Egypten**	[e'jyptǝn]
England	**England**	['ɛŋlʲand]
Estonia	**Estland**	['ɛstlʲand]
Finland	**Finland**	['finlʲand]
France	**Frankrike**	['fraŋkrike]
French Polynesia	**Franska Polynesien**	['franska pɔlʲy'nesiǝn]
Georgia	**Georgien**	[je'ɔrgiǝn]
Germany	**Tyskland**	['tʏsklʲand]
Ghana	**Ghana**	['gana]
Great Britain	**Storbritannien**	['stʊr‚bri'taniǝn]

Greece	**Grekland**	['grekl'and]
Haiti	**Haiti**	[ha'iti]
Hungary	**Ungern**	['uŋɛ:ŋ]

100. Countries. Part 2

Iceland	**Island**	['isl'and]
India	**Indien**	['indiən]
Indonesia	**Indonesien**	[indʊ'nesiən]
Iran	**Iran**	[i'ran]
Iraq	**Irak**	[i'rak]
Ireland	**Irland**	['il'and]
Israel	**Israel**	['israəl']
Italy	**Italien**	[i'taliən]

Jamaica	**Jamaica**	[ja'majka]
Japan	**Japan**	['japan]
Jordan	**Jordanien**	[jʊ:'daniən]
Kazakhstan	**Kazakstan**	[ka'sak‚stan]
Kenya	**Kenya**	['kenja]
Kirghizia	**Kirgizistan**	[kir'gisi‚stan]
Kuwait	**Kuwait**	[kʉ'vajt]

Laos	**Laos**	['l'aɔs]
Latvia	**Lettland**	['l'etl'and]
Lebanon	**Libanon**	['libanɔn]
Libya	**Libyen**	['libiən]
Liechtenstein	**Liechtenstein**	['lihtənstajn]
Lithuania	**Litauen**	[li'tauən]
Luxembourg	**Luxemburg**	['lʉksəm‚burj]

Macedonia (Republic of ~)	**Makedonien**	[make'dʊniən]
Madagascar	**Madagaskar**	[mada'gaskar]
Malaysia	**Malaysia**	[ma'l'ajsia]
Malta	**Malta**	['mal'ta]
Mexico	**Mexiko**	['mɛksikɔ]
Moldova, Moldavia	**Moldavien**	[mʊl'daviən]

Monaco	**Monaco**	['mɔnakɔ]
Mongolia	**Mongoliet**	[mʊngʊ'liet]
Montenegro	**Montenegro**	['mɔntə‚negrʊ]
Morocco	**Marocko**	[ma'rɔkʊ]
Myanmar	**Myanmar**	['mjanmar]

Namibia	**Namibia**	[na'mibia]
Nepal	**Nepal**	[ne'pal']
Netherlands	**Nederländerna**	['nedɛ:‚l'ɛndɛ:ŋa]
New Zealand	**Nya Zeeland**	['nya 'se:l'and]
North Korea	**Nordkorea**	['nʊ:d kʊ'rea]
Norway	**Norge**	['nɔrjə]

101. Countries. Part 3

Pakistan	**Pakistan**	['paki‚stan]
Palestine	**Palestina**	[palˈeˈstina]
Panama	**Panama**	['panama]
Paraguay	**Paraguay**	[parag'waj]
Peru	**Peru**	[pɛ'rʉ]
Poland	**Polen**	['pɔlˈen]
Portugal	**Portugal**	['pɔːtˌugalˈ]
Romania	**Rumänien**	[rʉ'mɛːniən]
Russia	**Ryssland**	['rʏslˈand]

Saudi Arabia	**Saudiarabien**	['saudi a'rabiən]
Scotland	**Skottland**	['skɔtlˈand]
Senegal	**Senegal**	[sene'galˈ]
Serbia	**Serbien**	['sɛrbiən]
Slovakia	**Slovakien**	[slˈɔ'vakiən]
Slovenia	**Slovenien**	[slˈɔ'veniən]

South Africa	**Republiken Sydafrika**	[repu'bliken 'syd‚afrika]
South Korea	**Sydkorea**	['syd‚kʉ'rea]
Spain	**Spanien**	['spaniən]
Suriname	**Surinam**	['sʉri‚nam]
Sweden	**Sverige**	['svɛrijə]
Switzerland	**Schweiz**	['ʃvɛjts]
Syria	**Syrien**	['syriən]

Taiwan	**Taiwan**	[taj'van]
Tajikistan	**Tadzjikistan**	[ta'dʒiki‚stan]
Tanzania	**Tanzania**	[tansa'nija]
Tasmania	**Tasmanien**	[tas'maniən]
Thailand	**Thailand**	['tajlˈand]
Tunisia	**Tunisien**	[tʉ'nisiən]
Turkey	**Turkiet**	[turkiet]
Turkmenistan	**Turkmenistan**	[turk'meni‚stan]

Ukraine	**Ukraina**	[u'krajna]
United Arab Emirates	**Förenade arabrepubliken**	[fø'renadə a'rab repub'likən]
United States of America	**Amerikas Förenta Stater**	[a'mɛrikas fø'rɛnta 'statər]
Uruguay	**Uruguay**	[ʉrug'waj]
Uzbekistan	**Uzbekistan**	[us'beki‚stan]

Vatican	**Vatikanstaten**	[vati'kan‚statən]
Venezuela	**Venezuela**	[venesu'ɛlˈa]
Vietnam	**Vietnam**	['vjɛtnam]
Zanzibar	**Zanzibar**	['sansibar]

Printed in Great Britain
by Amazon